MW00527693

THE LAST MIRACLE

My 18-Year Journey with the Amazin' New York Mets

THE LAST MIRACLE

My 18-Year Journey with the Amazin' New York Mets

Ed Kranepool

with Gary Kaschak

TRIUMPH
BOOKS

Library of Congress Cataloging-in-Publication Data available upon request

This book is available in quantity at special discounts for your group or organization. For further information, contact:

Triumph Books LLC
814 North Franklin Street
Chicago, Illinois 60610
(312) 337-0747
www.triumphbooks.com

Printed in U.S.A.
ISBN: 978-1-63727-270-1
Design by Nord Compo
Photos courtesy of Marc Levine unless otherwise indicated

Contents

Foreword

ED KRANEPOOL was already a 20-year-old major league veteran when I showed up at Shea Stadium in early April of 1965 as a wide-eyed, 20-year-old rookie on Opening Day. Casey Stengel was a manager in his 70s who would retire from the New York Mets after fracturing his hip just after the All-Star break. In spring training earlier that year, Stengel was reported to have told The Krane: "If you keep working at the things you're not good at, in 10 years you have a chance at being a superstar." The late Greg Goossen, a 19-year-old Mets prospect with a well-known taste for gin and late-night card games, said, "What about me, Casey?" To which Stengel replied, "Mr. Goossen, if you keep up the way you're going, in 10 years you got an outside shot at being 29."

It's a funny story but likely apocryphal. And Goose, a wonderful guy who did live hard, made it to the age of 65 while picking up some film credits along the way.

The new Mets mascot back then was dubbed Mr. Met and animated by an amazingly game young man named Dan Reilly, who romped around Shea Stadium in a Mets uniform topped with a huge, ungainly paper-mache head. Reilly, who worked in the Mets ticket department, lived with a couple of other fun-loving Irish guys downstairs from the first apartment that my wife, Cecelia, and I rented in Whitestone just a short hop from Shea Stadium. Reilly, who remained a lifetime friend, passed away a couple of years ago while the character he inhabited still exists today in Citi Field.

But I bring this up because when I think of Mr. Met, I think the title really belongs to Ed Kranepool. Who else arrived fresh out of James Monroe High School as a 17 year old and not only played a couple of games in 1962, but also spent his entire 18-year major league career with the franchise? Playing for a host of Mets managers from Stengel starting in 1962, the team's first season, through Gil Hodges, whom Kranepool replaced at first base in his first big league start, through Yogi Berra and later Joe Torre. In truth, Kranepool may not have become the superstar that Stengel suggested as a possibility, but I think he accomplished something even more difficult by keeping himself relevant through all those managers and general managers and through 18 seasons as a New York Met. No one will ever repeat that run so The Krane is my all-time Mr. Met.

It is still interesting to me how he and I gravitated together in the first place since we are very different people. I'm a bleeding-heart liberal, and The Krane is more conservative and can be a hard-nosed New Yorker. Just ask Tim Foli, a longtime big league shortstop, how far you can push The Krane. In the first of two stops with the Mets, Foli was a fiery, tough-on-himself young shortstop who was having a bad day at home plate and took it out to his position. When Krane was throwing him warmup grounders, Foli was angrily firing bullets back at Kranepool. Finally, The Krane refused to throw any to him, and when Foli confronted Kranepool in the Mets dugout, Foli ran into a hard left hand that knocked him out onto the dugout steps. Easy lesson there, which is further detailed in this book.

In 1969 we played in old Crosley Field in Cincinnati. I wasn't in the game so I had a good view from the dugout when it looked like the Mets had turned a 4-6-3 double-play to end the inning. The Krane was playing first base and, as was done then, he turned and handed the ball off to the Reds' first-base coach,

Jimmy Bragan. About that time it became clear that the second-base umpire was calling the runner safe because the shortstop had missed the base. The Krane turned to Bragan and says, "Gimme the fuckin' ball," which Bragan proceeded to throw down the right-field line. Upon which Kranepool grabbed him around the neck and dropped a couple of quick left hooks on his dome. Bragan later said, "I didn't think he was that strong." So, I always knew that you messed with The Krane at your own hazard.

But we roomed together at one point in my Mets career and always hung out together and never had a problem. I mean, in those days in the late 1960s, our motto seemed to be, "Win or lose, we will drink." I was very close to Tug McGraw, who never saw a shot of Irish whiskey he didn't like. Tug was on the 1969 World Series champion Mets team with Kranepool and me and later closed out the clinching game to give the Philadelphia Phillies their first ever World Series title in 1980. A writer once asked Tug what he did with his World Series bonuses, to which Tug replied, "I spent most of it on Irish whiskey and women. The rest of it I just pissed away." The three of us ran together a good bit. We didn't go looking for trouble, just a couple of pops to calm us down.

Later on, Kranepool and a friend of his from Amityville, Long Island, got the notion we should open a bar and restaurant. So we fronted a place called The Dugout on Route 110. Kranepool was way more of a business guy than I would ever be. I dropped out after a few years while Kranepool sold and bought back the building and finally sold it for good. The only thing I learned about the restaurant business was that I didn't know crap about it.

What's lasted between Kranepool and me has been our friendship. We've known one another for almost 70 years and we've shared a lot more than the championship rings we wear from 1969. His battle with type 1 diabetes and later the need for a new kidney was heroic to me. He never complained when it was clear he needed a new kidney. He just went about making it known because he knew at his age he needed someone to dedicate one of their kidneys to him. He made it happen, and it is one of the amazing stories he tells in this book—along with the ups and downs and trials and tribulations of an 18-year career with the Mets. In so many ways, including pecuniary and otherwise that The Krane may not even realize, he has been a more important friend to me than I have been to him. And for that I am grateful.

—Ron Swoboda
New York Mets outfielder, 1965–70

Introduction

THERE AREN'T MANY PEOPLE in our game who can say that they spent an entire career playing in one town with one team—especially a career of 18 years like I had. And there are just a few who played for their hometown team like I did. Lou Gehrig, another New Yorker like me, is the only other first baseman, who I can think of, who spent nearly two decades with a New York team. Had the circumstances been different for both of us, I'm sure we could have reached 20 years or more with that one club.

I read somewhere that the list of players with 10 or more years with one club is 187 and playing 20 or more years is just 17. Being tied for 27th place with nine others brings it home for me.

There's a lot that goes into achieving something like this. Of course, free agency didn't exist until late in my career, and if I could do it all over again, knowing how contracts exploded right after free agency, I may have hung on for a few more years. And maybe I would have signed with another club, who knows? Then Ed Kranepool's name would be out of this conversation of playing for one team an entire career, and it's something I'm pretty proud of and not that easy to have attained.

Maybe I'd never been traded, but I was in the conversation several times. The Mets had a revolving door of players from the time I came up in '62 to the time I left. There were a few times my name came up in trade talks for me to be thinking I should pack my bags. There were people in the organization who wanted me gone, and those that wanted me to stay. But somehow, through thick and thin, I survived all the talk and all the rumors and made it to the end as a Met for life.

It wasn't all that easy just staying a major leaguer. When I got sent down to the minors in 1970, a year after helping our club win the 1969 World Series, it was humiliating. I was still only 25 years old and wondering what I had to do to get back to the majors. I could have sulked and thrown a fit, but what good would come of that? So I fought through it and performed well in the minors. And when I came back up, I found a seat on the bench and hardly played at all, ending up with a ridiculous 47 at-bats that entire season. Suddenly, I knew I was going to be traded. It only made sense. Why keep me if you don't play me? After being promised by manager Joe Torre that I'd be the starting first baseman in 1978, I had 81 at-bats for the entire year. By then I'd established myself as the premier pinch-hitter in baseball, so they kept me around for that. But I still wanted to be an everyday player, not a pinch-hitter. Yet somehow, during that late stage of my career when my playing time went down to nothing, our other slugging first basemen like Donn Clendenon, John Milner, and Willie Montanez retired or got traded. And I was still standing, still a Met.

You know, my life as a New York Met had more twists and turns than you can imagine. But no matter where I go or who I run into, somebody always wants to talk to me about the '69 Mets. To think something so incredible like that magical 1969 season has carried on and still resonates with people is something that still amazes me to this day, and, honestly, I am very proud to have been part of it.

Players and coaches from the '69 team have been branded with a special seal that has stood the test of time and has defined each one of us forever. When you think about that, it's mind-boggling and humbling. As a Mets player representative for so many of those years, I'm confident speaking for my teammates from that club that we never grow tired hearing about or talking about the '69 Mets. I think the aura of the '69 Mets has something to do with the lack of technology and information, and the state of the world that seemed to draw people into the Mets by the millions.

It was a much simpler time for technology and for televised baseball games. Aside from watching home team games on stations like WOR or WPIX, there was just "The Game of The Week." And because of that, watching or seeing your favorite player perform—especially guys like Willie Mays and Henry Aaron—was a special moment. There was something special when the dominant players came into Shea. There was no highlight reel to see every day, no Top 10 plays of the day or anything like it. What you read about in the papers or *The Sporting News* gave you all you needed to know, so it was important to see these guys in person.

I've had countless conversations with fans who were 12, 13, 14 years old in 1969, who listened to our West Coast games late at night, covers up over their heads in bed, with transistor radios on, hoping their parents wouldn't discover what they were up to. And as radio signals went in and out like they sometimes do, important plays sometimes were missed, adding even more anxious moments. Sometimes the morning papers wouldn't even have the complete West Coast results. With no *SportsCenter* or instant results like we have today, that waiting period to see how the other clubs—especially the Cubs—had done added another exciting and nerve-racking element to the life of a fan.

Our nation was changing direction. Protests involving an unpopular Vietnam War. Woodstock. The assassinations of our president, John F. Kennedy, then later his brother Robert, and the Reverend Martin Luther King Jr. left a gaping hole in the pit of our collective stomachs. As we ached and cried and wondered what we could do to make things better, to make things right, many of us felt that we needed something good—something extraordinary—to help heal the hurt. We needed something to distract us. We needed a miracle. That's when we started winning. Nothing could ever replace that feeling we had that season, and nothing ever did.

That 1969 season came right smack in the middle of my career. I thought that all the losing ways were behind me, that I'd gone through my share of 100-loss seasons, and that we'd turned it around for good. I really believed we'd started a dynasty, that our pitching and defense and timely hitting and Gil Hodges would carry us for the next several years.

But baseball, like life, doesn't always work out that way. Injuries. Trades...the loss of Hodges. The rest of the league was out to get us. We hung in there for the next four years, then it all just changed following our World Series loss to the Oakland A's in 1973. And by the end of my playing career—the last four years or so—it felt to me like those early years again, only worse. The losing. The mismanagement. No direction. Bad trades. Bad contracts. Bad farm system. Lies. Loss of trust and integrity. No loyalty. Dwindling fan support.

I hope you enjoy my entire journey starting as that wide-eyed kid from the Bronx to the hobbled and hopefully wise sage I am today. As I think about that term "Miracle Mets," it doesn't come close to two more miracles that kept me and my wife alive some 50 years later.

—*Ed Kranepool*

Introduction

WHEN I WAS A BOY growing up in the Binghamton, New York, area in the mid-1960s, life for my two brothers and myself revolved around sports. Pickup football, basketball, and street hockey with neighborhood kids during the colder months was the norm. We watched the New York football Giants games on Sundays and listened to the radio as Marv Albert broadcast New York Knicks and Rangers games against an ever-crackling signal, fading, rising, and then fading again. Those ill-timed pauses added drama to any close game. And even though his words sometimes were muffled, his inflection—or lack thereof—gave us momentary hope or told another story.

As much as we loved playing those games, baseball was hands down the sport we loved the most. Anxious and excited, we couldn't wait for the season to start, to shed our scarves and mittens, to put away the pigskin and break down the hockey net, to oil up the glove and warm up the arm. Despite Mother Nature giving us four, maybe five good months to play ball, the cold and damp early months of spring did little to discourage us. The melting snow and above-freezing temperatures were a signal from somewhere good that the great baseball migration was at hand.

Of course, we dreamed about becoming professional ballplayers, producing impossibly amazing careers playing for our beloved New York Yankees, our names becoming synonymous with two of our heroes, Mickey Mantle and Roger Maris. I'd learned about both of them when I was six years old during that impossibly amazing 1961 season, at some point learning that the Yankees would be in the World Series every year. Like clockwork for the next four years, that lesson proved real until 1965. The bottom not only fell out, but it's also where the Yankees landed a year later. To see the Yankees finish last in 1966 followed by a one-notch rise a year later in the 10-team American League was unimaginable. As that awful truth settled in, another year went by, and my heroes like Mantle and Maris would soon be gone, too. So in 1969, at the tender age of 13, I decided it was time to follow the other New York team. I gave the Mets a chance.

It wasn't as if we couldn't root for both the Yankees and the Mets. They played in different leagues, and what one team did had no bearing on the other. So there was no chance of me becoming the Benedict Arnold of baseball. Perhaps my Yankees allegiance played a part in me pushing the Mets away. I never felt the connection like I had with my Yankees, and being that the Mets were a last-place team, I never gave them a chance. Oh, I knew their roster and I knew the stats of the players, but it was all from afar, as impersonal as it could be. So I decided to give them a chance.

Though I hadn't thought about it before helping write this book, handing that baton off from Mantle to the Mets seemed to be perfectly timed for a young fan like myself. And by season's end, with so many unbelievable games and so many unlikely heroes contributing in so many ways, I learned who they were. From Tom Seaver to Jerry Koosman to Duffy Dyer and Bud Harrelson, I knew them all. And while Mantle would forever remain my No. 1, the '69 Mets helped me get over what had happened to my Yankees. I'd become immersed in a season like no other.

As that '69 season moved into May and then into June, a few favorites emerged. It wasn't going to be easy replacing Maris and Mantle. But on my Mets, the two guys I cheered for the most and followed the most just happened to be Cleon Jones and Ed Kranepool. Jones was going to be the National League batting champion, and Kranepool was the powerful-hitting first baseman who reminded me of Mantle. In the end it didn't matter that Jones fell mere points short of that coveted title, or that Kranepool wasn't about to break any home run records. As I look back on it now, none of that mattered because in my ever-developing baseball mind I was understanding the rotation of baseball, the ebb and flow of a career, that players come and go, that teams you root for don't always win, and that there's plenty of room for new favorites like Jones and Kranepool.

Kranepool's story is one of survival—both in and out of baseball—how inexplicably he survived an 18-year career with one team with all its fits and starts, the benchings and demotions, the trades and trade rumors, and a revolving door in management and ownership. Although he'd be the first to tell you that the '69 Mets were a team full of miracles, the pair of life-threatening illnesses that both he and his wife, Monica, survived were the true miracles. It was a privilege to have worked with Jones on his book, *Coming Home*, and to collaborate with Kranepool, the second of my Mets heroes, on this book is hard to describe. Never did I imagine such opportunities, and looking back on it through the window of my 13-year-old self, well, it's impossibly amazing.

—*Gary Kaschak*

Chapter 1

PLAYGROUNDS
OF NEW YORK

GROWING UP IN THE '40S, the '50s, and into the early '60s was a time of significant change and transition for our country. Three wars, desegregation, nuclear threats, and so much more were just the tip of the iceberg. But I was just a kid back then, and kids I knew paid little attention to world events. And who knew that closer to home in the South Bronx, we had our own troubles brewing.

To say I was oblivious to what was going on around us—that is, the construction of the Cross Bronx Expressway—would be fair. As a 12 year old in 1955, I'd heard that the first part of the expressway opened, and while I had no idea what eminent domain meant, I knew enough. Neighborhoods had changed. Families had been displaced. Landlords and local business had disappeared, and more crimes were taking place. I read later on that its architect—Robert Moses—was the one responsible for displacing many thousands of people, houses of worship, and entire neighborhoods and found that quite ironic that a man named "Moses" could do such a thing. The impact from all that may have been just a few miles away from us, but I don't recall feeling much about any of it, knowing our Castle Hill neighborhood and especially Castle Hill Playground had been spared.

I've always said that timing is everything, and this was one of those times. Had that expressway path been in another direction, our neighborhood may have been in the rubble, and if that had happened, I never would have become a major league ballplayer.

But the worries of such things would come much later for me in my life. I was just a boy who wanted to play baseball. I wanted to know how many homers Mickey Mantle and Roger Maris hit last night or how far ahead the Yankees were in the standings. I wanted to know when I could go to another game at the stadium and to plan on having enough change in my pockets to afford a hot dog or two.

When I got some free tickets from the *Journal-American*, I went to a New York Yankees game. Anytime I could go see the Yankees, I would sit out in the right field bleachers hoping to catch a ball from Mickey Mantle or Roger Maris. Those were my Yankee years growing up, those late '50s and early '60s when they were winning pennants every year. It was natural for me to be a Yankees fan, not only because they won all the time, but also because Yankee Stadium was so close to us. Like so many of us back then, we loved Mantle, and I was one of them who really idolized him. He was my favorite player by far, and I had imagined myself playing with Mantle as his teammate one day.

That was right around the same time I became interested in baseball cards. I didn't collect cards like a lot of guys did, but I scaled them, I flipped them and put them in the spokes of my bike, especially any of the Yankees cards and most especially Mantle. None of us were smart enough to save them or keep them in good condition, or knew the value they'd have in the future. Once you outgrew something, your mother would throw it out. I probably had Mantle's rookie card back then, maybe had more than one. Who the hell knows?

The neighborhood around Yankee Stadium wasn't the greatest, and neither was ours. Our struggles were the same or even greater than most every family around. That's because my mom was living off a military pension after they killed my dad in the war three months before I was born. He was gunned down by the Germans in France. I found out soon enough that living off a military pension wasn't enough to support a family. That is a sad statement. You die for your country, and your family still struggles.

But we never gave it much thought that the struggle was that unusual. It was just a way of life for us and for our neighbors. Rarely did we venture too far from our neighborhood and never took a real vacation. We didn't have any rich friends or knew anyone who lived in a mansion or who drove a fancy car. Our world was the world as we knew it.

The neighborhood was a collection of apartments and three family homes with very little property in between. We lived in a three-family apartment that we shared with two other families that was surrounded by a small building, a store in the front, a shoemaker, and more apartments around us. Buildings and residences were like that all the way down from where we lived on Castle Hill and as far as the eye could see. Further down, they built subsidized apartments for low to middle-income people, and that meant we were better off than some of those families that lived there. Even when we explored some other neighborhood, it all seemed the same. This was the inner city of the Bronx, where over a million and a half people lived in an area of 70 square miles. Looking back on it now, it wasn't the ghetto, but not that great of an area either.

There were families all over the place, some with 10 kids in a household. We had a melting pot of race, religion, color; you name it. And with such tight quarters and the daily pressures of life just trying to get by and making some sense of it all, you could hear the arguments or see the fights coming from the streets or even from inside the homes. Despite all the problems that came with living like most of us did, families were intact. Oh, I'm sure there were a few absentee fathers and other things going on behind the scenes, but I don't remember any of my friends not having a father to grow up with.

I never felt sorry for myself not having a dad. I never dwelled on it or complained or even got mad at the world. It would have changed if he had been alive for me to know him. But even after all this time, I never looked into his life. Of course, Mom would mention him from time to time, but I never felt curious to know more. I don't know if that's a good thing or a bad thing. All I know is I never pursued his past.

In time, the closest person I had to a father growing up was our next-door neighbor, Jimmy Schiafo. Schiafo was my first coach in Little League and, despite having two boys the same age as I was, he took me under his wing and made sure we all worked out together. He'd take me outside where he'd pitch to me, and while I didn't know it then, he was more of a batting coach than I'd ever had in the majors. He did some unique things, like filling up a bucket of water and placing it down in front of my right foot to keep me from "stepping in the bucket" when I swung the bat. Schiafo understood the art of hitting and made sure I was picking up on everything he was teaching. I think he took extra time to develop me as a hitter and I always gave him credit for that. When his wife died, I thought he and my mom would get married, but it never happened.

Growing up in the city doesn't afford you many opportunities to do something fun, and unless you were lucky enough like I was to live a stone's throw away from Castle Hill Playground, you could easily get into trouble. Castle Hill was our retreat, our haven for just about anything.

Without that park being as close as it was, I don't know what I would have done with myself. I spent my entire summers there, as did most of the neighborhood kids. There were a million things to do to keep you out of trouble, and there was trouble with all the gangs around. We lived, slept, and thought about the playground all the time. I was there from sunup to sundown and would run home at noon to have lunch because I was only a block away, and that made it easy. All I knew was that park.

My mother was strict about eating three meals a day, and off I'd go to the park right after breakfast, then home again for a quick lunch, then back to the playground as fast as I could because I didn't want to miss any of the action. I mentioned it earlier, and this is no stretch when I say this, but I owe my entire baseball career to Castle Hill Playground. It's where I developed and learned most of my baseball skills.

We never went away in the summer to any of those fancy camps, and they sure didn't have any camps in the Bronx either. Being as poor as we were, we didn't play the fancy sports like tennis or golf because we couldn't afford tennis rackets or golf clubs. Even if we could, we'd learned by playing team sports and liked them much better. You played basketball because all you needed was a basketball. You played baseball or stickball because we could afford it. And we never played Wiffle Ball because we thought that was more of a sissy game, anyway.

The park was your typical playground designed with handball courts, swing sets, slides, and a recreational area with spigots built into the ground that shot water high into the air to help you cool off under the sweltering sun. And being that we were running around all day long in the New York heat, we used those to cool off all the time. On the other side, six basketball courts were always active with games or a guy or two playing horse or going one-on-one with each other. They had two softball fields that were made of blacktop, so we were always skinning our knees or cutting our hands when we fell. Of course, we couldn't play baseball or stickball all the time. In the winter they had an area inside the clubhouse where we could play shuffleboard, and they flooded out an area for ice skating as well, so there was something to do year-round.

We'd choose up sides for our baseball games and on those rare times when we didn't have enough players to form a complete nine-man team, we'd eliminate the right fielder or something like that, then learn not to hit it there. I guess you could say it was when you learned to pull the ball or go ups the middle with it. Sometimes we had only a few guys around and when we only had two guys, you played a game we called, "Fast pitch," where you drew a box on the wall of the handball courts, and that box became the strike zone. Of course, you stole your mother's broomstick for your stickball bat and used those pinky Spalding balls that cost less than a quarter back then.

Every reputation begins somewhere, and mine began with playing stickball, or some improvised version of it. We learned to improvise rules of the game by what we had to work with. For us, there were three fences that ran back to back, about 20 feet apart, that seemed perfect for our scoring. Hitting one over the closest fence was a double, a triple over the middle fence, and a home run over the farthest fence. I got a reputation for being a great stickball player not only because I was a great hitter, but I also did an odd thing by always choosing to bat first.

As my reputation spread, I was even being treated special by the local gangs, and there were plenty of them and plenty of opportunities in the Bronx to get yourself in trouble. My sister was three years older than I and she knew a lot of those boys because they were her age. But those gangs treated me well. They didn't allow me to stay with them or hang out with them, and it's a good thing because those fellows got in trouble a lot. They'd push me home and they didn't want me to stay around and hangout on the corners at night because they wanted me to play on their softball team or their stickball team. I was that good of a player to them, and they were out to protect me and give themselves an advantage in our games. Later on when I became a New York Mets player, I'd run into one of them at a Mets game where they'd yell out their names, wanting to be recognized. Maybe I didn't always pick up on it right away, but I finally did, and we'd have a talk where they'd remind me how right they were.

They used to always think it was strange that I'd choose to bat first because that went against the norm we'd learned about baseball. Hitting last gave you that last opportunity as the home player where a lot of games were decided, but I discovered early on, and so did my friends, that I wasn't an easy out. Sometimes a regulation three-out inning would take five or 10 minutes, sometimes 15, but most of my innings when I batted lasted a half hour or more. What that meant was an opposing pitcher getting a sore arm after just an inning. As the game moved on and my innings lasted a half hour each, his arm grew wearier and couldn't last a full nine, resulting in a lopsided win for me.

When we first started playing Little League, somebody donated some property next to an oil company, and the plows just flattened it out, put up a backstop that said, "That's Little

League." It was all dirt with no grass or fences in the out-field, but just having baselines and bases made it feel like we were playing in the majors, which was a big step up from the blacktop we'd played on before. My mom came to every game of my Little League, but it was tough on her. She would drive to the games and sometimes go right back after the games to some odd job she was doing. She followed me right to the major leagues and was there with Schiafo at my workouts for the Mets at the Polo Grounds and later when the Mets signed me.

I had my first real setback my second year of Little League when I fractured the elbow on my throwing arm. While playing stickball in the dark on one of those black-topped courts, some guy tripped me when I was trying to score. I fell and slammed my elbow, breaking it. It was never right after that.

That was tough on me because I was a pitcher back then and owned my share of pitching records, including a couple of no-hitters. I think most kids would have given up and let the bone heal, but that wasn't me. I couldn't imagine missing an entire season, let alone a single inning, so I taught myself to throw right-handed. It wasn't easy, but I was determined and had set my mind on it. After all the practicing and repetitions throwing with my opposite hand, it was good enough, so they put me back at first base. I adjusted to it well, but I didn't have the speed or control to take the mound. I was lucky that the break was in such a place that it didn't affect my swinging the bat, so I went out and hit .700.

It always surprised people when I state some fact or sta-tistic from a game played long ago or remember what some player did or certain game situations. Even now I have little trouble remembering stuff like that. So I'm not picking a random number when I say I batted .700 and did for all three years of Little League.

My elbow never healed, so I pitched only a few games my last year in Little League. I never had surgery to repair it, and it still bothers me sometimes. And I feel that if that injury hadn't occurred, I could have been a pitcher and a fielder and they could have been talking about Ed Kranepool like they talk about Shohei Ohtani. Who knows?

Once I finished Little League, I joined up with the sandlot teams that played all around the different boroughs but mostly in the Bronx. That first year when I was 13, the field dimensions were longer than Little League but didn't go to full regulation baseball dimensions for my age group. But that mattered little because I ended up playing with the older guys anyway on the normal dimensions, and had to get used to it, which I did right from the start.

There was a Babe Ruth League and a lot of other leagues in the Bronx, but I liked sandlot baseball the most. I think the better players played sandlot, and that's where I wanted to be. It doesn't sound very organized, but it was with schedules and teams that we played throughout the Bronx and even near Yankee Stadium at Frank Frisch Field. There were a lot of fields around and we played doubleheaders on the weekends. Two games on Saturday, a couple more on Sunday, and sometimes I'd play for another team, giving me sometimes five games on a weekend. That still wasn't enough for me. I couldn't get enough baseball.

Before sandlot I used to go to our Presbyterian church every Sunday and to Sunday school, but with the doubleheaders scheduled on Sundays, I had to give up something and I gave up going to church. Some people today would question that, but games started early and went into the afternoon.

After a few years playing sandlot, I made the roster of our Monroe High School team as a 10th grader. Contrasted by the sizable crowds that came to our sandlot games, hardly any students came to watch us in high school. Maybe it was because baseball in the Bronx was not a great spectator sport in high school or that they played the games in the afternoon right after school when people were still working or the students were going home. High school basketball and football drew all the crowds. So the few people that would come out were mostly scouts—guys they called "bird dogs"—people who worked for the ballclubs that would call in their regular scouts if they noticed somebody special.

Between sandlot and high school, I began recognizing the so-called bird dog scouts coming out to see me play. Bird dogs were the scouting party for the real scouts, local guys who worked for the ballclubs who would call in their regular scouts if they noticed somebody special. We played 70-to-80 sandlot games over the summer and 20 in high school, so there was a lot of baseball to be seen and observed and a lot of bird scouts hanging around the backstop and down the lines. I hit over .500 for some of those years, so as I got better and more scouts came to our games, I started looking for them in the stands and started thinking for the first time I could make it to the big leagues.

And Schiafo was there all the time, looking out for me. When the scouts wanted to learn more about me, they'd search out for Schiafo. They weren't allowed to say much to any player who hadn't graduated from high school or risk getting in trouble. They may have asked you a few questions or made some comment, but it was very casual conversation and never crossed that line about signing or talking about money or whatever.

Back in those days, you could deal with any ballclub you wanted to because there was no draft, so you just signed with whatever team you wanted to. As the bird dogs got the word out on me, the real scouts from most teams came around to see me play.

Chapter 2

GRADUATING TO LIFE

I'D SAY I WAS AN AVERAGE STUDENT in high school, and by average I mean C+. I wasn't much for studying and since I played both basketball and baseball in high school, I'd rather be on the hardcourt or on the diamond than studying for some test.

I was the happiest playing baseball and basketball. So when they gave us the option when I was a freshman to sign up for regular gym class or for swimming lessons, I think I surprised a lot of people when I signed up for swimming. My sister had a pass to the community swimming pool in the Bronx, but for some reason, I never went with her. I thought this would be the perfect opportunity for me to learn how to swim, so I signed up for swimming.

After about two or three swimming lessons the varsity basketball coach, Sam Tolkoff, had been looking around for me, wondering why I wasn't participating in the regular gym classes. Being that basketball was being played in the regular gym class, he was thinking ahead and knew I was a good overall athlete and would make a good basketball player. So he came down to the pool area and saw me in the pool, being taught with the other students. He said, "What the hell are you doing down here?" I replied, "I was taking up swimming. I never learned how and wanted to." He said, "You don't need this. Go upstairs to the gym." And so I did. He made me leave the swimming class just when I was getting to like it. He was protecting his own interests and I hold no ill-feelings for that. In fact, we became very good friends and still are today, and I did become a good basketball player under his guidance. I developed each year and got better and better, got stronger and taller.

But I never learned how to swim and still don't know how. It's probably the biggest disappointment I had in high school. I said many, many times to my wife that I never took advantage of James Monroe High's swimming classes and over the years I've had many, many boats and never could go swimming with the kids because I couldn't jump off the boat without a life jacket. By then, everybody in the family became good swimmers but me. On vacation when everybody else was snorkeling, I wouldn't go because I wasn't comfortable in the water. I had houses with indoor swimming pools, but I still never learned. I was always so busy tied up in baseball that it just passed me by and all these years later I still can't swim. And I regret it.

By the time I was a junior, I'd filled out to 6'3" or 6'4" and weighed about 210. By then, Tolkoff tutored me in basketball and made me into a pretty good shooter and defensive player, good enough to draw the attention of the college scouts. In my senior year, I set a school basketball record by averaging about 24 points per game. And because of that, there were quite a few offers from the colleges, major colleges like North Carolina and St. John's. I listened to their offers, but basketball had always been more for staying in shape, and from Day One, I always knew I wanted to play professional baseball.

I was the perfect size for football, but we had a bad team, and there was always that chance of getting hurt. I don't think being a bad team had anything to do with my decision not to play because I saw the way guys were being hit and the injuries that were occurring. But the football coach told me he'd make me a defensive end, and because of my size, there was little chance of getting seriously hurt. He tried several times to change my mind, but I never budged. I know I could have been a good football player, but I made the right decision by not playing. Our baseball co-captain, Donnie Novick, decided to play football, and they made him into an end. And guess what? He tore up his knee in a game, and like my elbow injury, it never mended properly.

Novick was a great baseball player who led the country in hitting when he went to New York University after graduation from high school. But because of that football injury, it affected him when he went to the minor leagues to play baseball. He couldn't get a contract after that.

Monroe was really known for baseball back then, and our school trophy case held plenty of photos, balls, and banners celebrating many championships. Our infield at the time was nicknamed, "The Million Dollar Infield," with me, Alan Feldstein, John Melarczik, and Steve Russo named to the all-city team. They always loved baseball at Monroe, and we always qualified for the playoffs and the championships the three years I was there. We never won the championship, but as a junior, we finished second, losing a playoff game when one of our fielders dropped a pop-up with the bases loaded to one of the teams from Queens. There were two outs, and they ran on contact and scored their three runs on that dropped fly ball to beat us 3–2.

My final game as a senior had a similar heartbreaking storyline, a 6–5 loss in the Public School Athletic League (PSAL) championship game to Curtis High School. I pitched the final three innings in relief, but earlier, I tripped over a garden hose chasing down a fly ball in right field that allowed two runs to score. It's hard to believe no one saw that hose before or during the game, and I wonder to this day what the outcome of that game would have been had I caught that ball and not tripped. At any rate, it stung to lose games in such ways. And even though we lost that game, comparisons to great major league ballplayers had been made to me, and expectations were running high.

When I entered my senior year with 10 career high school home runs, I trailed Monroe's legendary player and Cooperstown Hall of Famer, Hank Greenberg, by eight homers. I knew I had a chance for the record. I wasn't really concentrating on the record; I just wanted to win. But as I kept depositing balls for home runs to deep right-center beyond a tree the students named, "Eddies' Tree," I clubbed my 19th home run late in the year and passed Greenberg's record he set in 1929. That's when things started to get a little crazy.

I wouldn't say there was a bidding war for my services because the New York Mets hands down were the team showing the most interest. Right from the start, Mets scout Bubber Jonnard had been at most of my games for those three years, taking notes and reporting back to the Mets brass. Jonnard was easily the most recognizable scout because he was always at the games, come rain or shine. You could just tell he was champing at the bit for graduation day to come when teams could legally offer me a contact. But like anything else with a good product, competition was right around the corner.

I was being compared to Greenberg a lot from both the press and the locals. They always compare. And now that I'd surpassed his home run record at Monroe, people were beginning to talk about me as a sure Hall of Famer like Greenberg had become. It felt nice to hear all the talk, and being just 17, I was starting to imagine myself being as good or better than he was.

Greenberg had become an executive with the Chicago White Sox and was friendly with Monroe's athletic director, Steve Ray, who was also a scout for the White Sox. Ray had the inside track on my makeup and character and had attended all of our high school games and was at many of our practices, so there was a solid connection, to say the least. And I'd met Greenberg a few times on his visits to the school, so I knew the White Sox were very interested in me. Even with the relationship I had with Ray, I felt no moral obligation to tender a contract with the White Sox and was really looking for the best deal and the best opportunity to get to the major leagues.

The White Sox roster sported a young outfield and an older first baseman. Once you hit 30, that was an unofficial signal that you were starting to be over the hill. But Joe Cunningham was having a decent year as their first baseman. Cunningham was about to turn 30, so he might have had a few good years ahead of him, but that was it. The Sox outfield of Floyd Robinson, Jim Landis, and Mike Hershberger were all fairly young, but their bench and utility players was questionable.

Adding to the mix, the New York Yankees were my team and had me in for a tryout when I was a junior. I always wanted to be a Yankee because they were my favorite team, and what kid doesn't dream of playing for his favorite team, especially his hometown team? My heart was going in that direction, but I had to be careful with my decision.

But I heard so many stories about the Yankees having so many great players in the minor leagues who got lost in the mix because of all the talent they had throughout the minor league system and onto the major league roster. As good as you are when you sign, you find out you're not as good as you think you are, and before long, you're just another player in their system, being traded, released, or doomed to the minors your whole career.

And they were in the World Series every year and still fairly young. I knew their lineup by heart and knew it would be a tough one to break into, let alone make the roster. Bill Skowron had made the All-Star team five years in a row as a first baseman, so I wasn't about to take his place. Plus, they had a young Joe Pepitone waiting in the wings. Roger Maris was over in right field, and we all know what he had done. Mickey Mantle was in center and he wasn't being replaced by anyone. Plus, I was no center fielder. My only true shot was left field. But they had Hector Lopez, Yogi Berra, and Rookie of the Year Tommy Tresh out there. With Tony Kubek being recalled by the National Guard, Tresh played mostly shortstop during the season, but it was still Kubek's job when he came back. I figured once Kubek came back they'd want to keep Tresh's bat in the lineup. With Bobby Richardson having a hold on second base and Clete Boyer another fixture at third, the only logical place to put Tresh was in left field. Maybe the Yankees would sign me, but the road to the majors was full of traffic. The Mets, on the other hand, seemed liked the best opportunity to make the major leagues roster sooner rather than later.

I opened up the paper about a week before graduation and knew the Mets had won a day game against Milwaukee at the Polo Grounds. Their lineup that day featured 39-year-old Gene Woodling in left and 38-year-old Gil Hodges replacing 28-year-old Marv Throneberry at first. Younger guys like Joe Christopher and Jim Hickman rounded out the outfield, but neither player was having a good year. Other outfielders on the roster like Richie Ashburn weren't getting any younger. That's when I could see myself making the club, being a starter and proving people right in what they saw in me.

I got myself pretty geared up for June 27th, graduation day. It certainly wasn't going to be your usual graduation day spent with friends and family celebrating a milestone. I was 17 years of age, about to sign a major league contract, and life was going to change on the spot for me and my family.

When the doorbell rang that night, our first meeting was with Jonnard and Mets vice president Johnny Murphy. Since Jonnard had made the biggest effort in signing me, I gave him and the Mets the first shot at an offer. Murphy asked me how much I thought the contract should be, but what do I know? I heard that Tommie Agee had gotten $60,000 with the Cleveland Indians but thought I could do better. So I kept my cool, and asked for $80,000. That kind of got the ball rolling. Add in some decent incentives for making Double A, Triple A, and the major league team.

As a formality we spoke to the White Sox, but I didn't want to leave New York. I told the White Sox and Ray what the offer was, and he said he couldn't match it. And just like that I was a New York Met.

From my own point of view I thought it was a good baseball decision. The Mets were a New York team, I wanted to stay in New York and to be part of something new and exciting. The Mets had a new stadium in the works. They had Casey Stengel as their manager. And even though I had never been a Brooklyn Dodgers or New York Giants fan, I thought it would be fun to be part of making their old fans happy again.

I only had one thought in mind playing in the major leagues, and that's playing at home. You don't realize it at the time how much more difficult it was going to be to playing at home in New York rather than if I signed with the White Sox club. In hindsight, I'm pretty sure I wouldn't have put as much pressure on myself.

When I got my signing bonus, nobody in the neighborhood or any of our relatives really bothered me for money. You hear about such things all the time: when somebody comes into some money, suddenly everybody's your friend. But that didn't happen. I was so busy, and everything was happening so fast that I had to get myself packed and take care of a few things because two days after signing my contract I was on a plane headed for the West Coast as a Met.

That's one of the many things I thought about on that plane ride to California. It was almost hard to imagine that I'd graduated from high school and signed a major league contract on the same day, and 48 hours later, I'm taking the first plane ride in my life and really the first time I'd been anywhere outside of the Bronx.

Of course, I was thinking about actually playing when I got there, imagining myself hitting a home run in my first at-bat, that kind of thing. But the other thoughts were there, too, like striking out or making an error or a base running mistake. I'd already put some pressure on myself, but it was a six-hour flight with plenty of time to think of such things. And you couldn't help but think about the signing bonus and what to do with the money. But I knew all along I'd buy a house for my mother, and that's what I did—a nice home out in White Plains where we lived there together for the first couple of years that I played.

Chapter 3

GROWING UP AGAIN

WHEN WE LANDED IN LOS ANGELES, the New York Mets sent their traveling secretary to pick me up at the airport and whisked me off to Dodger Stadium to work out with the team before the game. With all the publicity I'd been getting from the press back home after signing with the Mets and now this, I was feeling like a celebrity.

I got dressed in the clubhouse and took a good look around at all the lockers of the players. In just a few minutes, I'd be going out to the dugout and onto the field to meet Casey Stengel and my new teammates. To say I was nervous would be an understatement. I spotted Stengel right away, and he welcomed me and introduced to me to all the players. He said, "Here's our new rookie that we just signed," and that was that.

That was a strange sort of feeling, shaking hands with guys I admired and only could see from afar. I mean, there were Gil Hodges and Richie Ashburn and other guys wishing me luck and patting me on the back. And now we were teammates. I was a bit starstruck but never showed that to them. And I was equally in awe of the Dodgers ballpark. I'd never seen such a beautiful place before. Of course, I loved Yankee Stadium, but this ballpark had so many great views and was as new as it gets.

Stengel worked me out at first base, taking grounders as was usual in any level of play. I was nervous, and there I was, throwing ground balls to Felix Mantilla, Elio Chacon, and Rod Kanehl. I still found that hard to believe as I took their throws and squeezed the glove extra hard to make sure no ball would flop out onto the field. I was so nervous; my knees were shaking, and I was hoping no one would notice. But after a while, my nerves settled down, and I kept my focus on each throw. But I hadn't focused enough, and because of it, I almost got hurt during that workout.

As a first baseman, it was my responsibility to set up one of those screens they used on each base to protect the infielders from getting hit with a line drive or a ground ball by the guys taking batting practice. We never had screens in high school or on the sandlot, so I placed the screen where I thought it should go in front of me at the bag.

On one of the throws from Chacon, one of the lefty hitters at the batting cage lined a hard grounder that hooked around the screen and got me good on my thigh, about two inches from my private parts. When I got back to the clubhouse, Stengel said, "You better wear a cup from now on," and had a good laugh about it. "You don't want to ruin your career before it even starts." I followed his advice and now I wear a cup even when I'm watching a game on TV!

Stengel posted the lineup earlier, and I knew my name wasn't going to be on it. Unlike today when a manager puts a new guy into the lineup right away, Stengel wasn't about to do that. He wanted me to sit next to him during the game and observe what was happening, to get a feel for a major league game. Of course I was disappointed, but with Sandy Koufax taking the mound, Stengel's lineup was all righties except leadoff hitter Ashburn, who was hitting .330 and on his way to another great year.

Koufax hadn't quite yet become the dominant pitcher he'd end up being and had lost his last two starts against the Milwaukee

Braves and Cincinnati Reds. I recalled that about a month earlier, when he pitched against the Mets at the Polo Grounds, he got roughed up pretty good. He ended up winning that game, but the Mets broke through against him, scoring six runs on 13 hits, something that didn't happen too often in any game.

I'd read the sports page on the plane ride and took a good look at the Mets game and its box score. The Mets had put together a rather strange game, scoring 10 runs on just four hits—which is another oddity in baseball. The highlights of the game came mostly in the first inning when the Mets scored six times on seven walks and just one hit off of Joe Moeller and Ron Perranoski. Later in the game, Stan Williams walked another eight guys, and by games end, the Los Angeles Dodgers had surrendered an amazing 16 walks for the game. Couple that with the San Francisco Giants win against the Philadelphia Phillies, that dropped the Dodgers a half game behind the Giants for first place in the standings. With the Mets looking to gain some respect with at least a split of the four-game series, I'm sure the Dodgers were looking to not be embarrassed with another loss, especially on their home turf.

The series was knotted at a game each, but winning two in a row was a rare accomplishment for the Mets. I'd followed them closely even before I signed and knew they'd had an 17-game losing streak and hadn't won two in a row in over three weeks. I'd always played on winning teams my whole life and wondered what that felt like to be 20–52, losing all the time and to be so far out of first place entrenched in last place at mid-season. I wondered what guys like Hodges and Gene Woodling were thinking, guys who'd played on winning teams before, and how they were handling playing for the worst team in baseball. There was a lot of season left, and hopefully I'd be around to find out myself how it felt. It seemed like as good a time as any to gain a little respect in a lost season and try to dig our way out of the cellar.

Those baseball oddities from just two recent games the Mets played against the Dodgers were about to change as Koufax took the mound. I watched his warmups, and he looked sharp to me.

I sat alongside of Stengel during the game and was in awe of Koufax. He struck out the side in the first inning, making it look easy. And as the game went on and into the later innings, Koufax seemed just as sharp or sharper than he looked earlier. In the ninth inning, he still had his no-hitter going when Stengel took a look up and down the dugout for a pinch-hitter. I think the two guys on the bench were myself and Woodling, and we were both left-handed hitters. I had a fleeting thought that Stengel would send me in. And wouldn't that be the headline if some 17-year-old phenom got the base hit to break up the no-hitter? But it didn't happen that way. Stengel told Woodling to "Grab a bat," and Koufax promptly walked him. Three ground-outs later, Koufax had his first no-hitter.

The next day, I got to see Don Drysdale pitch, and even though he didn't toss a no-hitter, I marveled at his game. And just like Koufax had done the night before, Drysdale struck out 13 Mets in an easy 5–1 win. After watching two games from the dugout, I started to wonder if the whole league was like this with such great pitchers, and if it was, I was in trouble.

Sitting next to Stengel for those two games, I really paid attention to the game and I noticed there were some glaring differences between the two ballclubs. The Dodgers had speed and power and young rising stars like Frank Howard, Tommy and Willie Davis, and a basestealer named Maury Wills. Whenever they got a man on base, there was a good chance somebody was gonna go. Even their catcher, Johnny Roseboro, was a threat and stole a base in one of the games I watched. Wills had one stolen base to get him over 40 for the year, and Tommy Davis knocked in a few more runs to get him to 81. Being that this was the exact halfway point of the season, who knew if they could maintain such a pace. I couldn't imagine a better club in the league as we headed to San Francisco to play the Giants.

I stayed with the team for their next series in San Francisco, but didn't play at all, not even to pinch hit or go in for defense. I can't say I was surprised, but being blown out in three games, I think they could have put me in. But Stengel stuck to his guns and had me right next to him on the bench as an observer. Of course, I was anxious to see Willie Mays and Orlando Cepeda perform, but it wasn't just those guys that were having a great season. They had six guys in the lineup who were all over .300 and they did it with power. The Mets took the opener, then gave up double-digit runs in each of the three losses that followed.

I paid particular attention to their rising star, Willie McCovey, especially after the seven RBIs he had in one of those games. McCovey had played some first base and mostly outfield, so I could see myself in him. Not in the sense of the power he had, but fitting in with the Mets as an outfielder/first baseman and playing every day in the near future.

I had a lot on my mind as they put me on a plane to Syracuse to join up with the Syracuse Chiefs Triple A ballclub. I did what I could to find out more about the team, but all I'd really been told was that I'd be playing regularly and the manager's name was Frank Verdi. I knew I'd be joining another losing team with no real stars or name players on the roster, so I felt there was another advantage in getting to the Mets sooner rather than later.

In my first minor league game, I went up against 40-year-old Max Surkont, a journeyman pitcher trying to hang on and get back up to the majors. Surkont had played eight seasons in the minor leagues before getting his chance with the Chicago White Sox, then moved around a dozen times or so between the majors and the minors. The fact that he hadn't played in the majors in over five years didn't seem to affect his competitive spirit. Lots of the old guys like Surkont had long careers in the minor leagues. Triple A back in those days was good baseball, with a lot of ex-major leaguer's holding on. And it was good, highly competitive baseball.

As a kid, I would always dig in like you always see guys do. I remember digging in with Surkont on the mound, my head was down, not paying attention to anything other than my cleat. Before you know it, I heard the umpire yell out, "Strike!" I never saw the Goddamned thing, but I heard it. I looked back at the catcher holding the ball, and he just kind of smirked and showed me the ball. I was surprised and thought he could have hit me in the head because he didn't have good control. I looked out at the mound, and Surkont was ready to go with another pitch, nodding and letting me know who the boss was. Surkont was basically saying to me, "Get ready, kid, or you're gonna get hit in the head."

I learned a valuable lesson after Surkont fast pitched me, and it stayed with me my entire career. They'd pull these kinds of things on young players like myself. These old-time veterans knew all the tricks. They knew I was a young kid who'd signed a big contract and they wanted to prove a point. I was on their turf and needed to prove myself to them. Nothing was going to come easy.

After just a couple of weeks of me playing for the Syracuse Chiefs, Mets vice president Johnny Murphy flew in to Syracuse to meet with me. He told me that the first baseman for the Knoxville Smokies of the South Atlantic League had gotten hurt, and they wanted me to take his place and get more experience in another league. I knew I'd struggled in the 14 games I played for the Chiefs, but this seemed like a demotion. Murphy convinced me it was the best thing for me and for the organization, so I packed my bags and hopped on another plane to Knoxville.

I don't think Murphy and the Knoxville manger, Frank Carswell, were on the same page or even discussed my situation because when I arrived in town, Carswell asked, "What are you doing down here with the Mets?" I said they sent me down here to fill in for somebody. He just kind of looked at me as if I had two heads and emphasized that, "This was a Detroit chain, and I'm only gonna play the Detroit players." Well, I told him all I knew was what Murphy had told me. And that was that.

About three weeks went by and Carswell had softened a bit. He'd told me from the start I wasn't going to play, but he was good enough to come out every afternoon and pitch batting practice to me. He must have seen something in me because he put me into seven games. But I batted only 20 times—a far cry from the guy who was supposed to be playing every day.

I had assumed that Murphy knew what was going on in Knoxville after I arrived, and it turns out, he didn't. When he came down and found out how little I'd been used, he seemed surprised, and that was a surprise to me. I guess I assumed there was communication from one front office to the other, but that didn't happen. I guess they didn't follow up on me too much, and being so young, I didn't know any better. I wasn't going to question anybody and was still learning the ropes. So Murphy made some calls, and it was decided I'd join the Auburn, New York club in the New York Penn League—the lowest minor league level there was.

There were about three weeks left in their season, and I got plugged right into first base for the last 20 games of the year. I think their regular first baseman had gotten injured, so that helped to know I'd be in there every day. And it felt good on a club battling for a playoff position. I ended up batting around .350, and we ended up winning the championship. With just a week or so to go in the major leagues, the Mets called me up for the final week of the season.

It was an experience for me to travel around like that because I never left the Bronx before. Before I left for Los Angeles on my first flight, I didn't know how to travel. I didn't know how to do anything at 17. And there I was, traveling around the United States, playing on three teams and on the roster of a fourth. When it was all said and done, I'd reached .300 with all my combined minor league totals, won a championship, and got to see the country and how different things were outside of New York.

As I got on another plane to meet the Mets in New York for their final week of the season, I had some thoughts about what I'd experienced—especially things in the South that I saw during my brief stay at Knoxville. My first day there when I met the team in Savannah, Georgia, was the first time I saw major, major racism. After checking into our hotel and getting unpacked, I wanted to check out the area, walk around, and get accustomed to my surroundings. As I was taking a walk down one of the neighborhood streets, I heard someone whistling then yelling, "Hey, boy!" I didn't know what the hell was going on in because back home in New York people don't talk to one another on the streets. And I heard again, "Hey boy. You're on the wrong side of the street." I didn't know what the hell he was talking about, but I knew he was talking to me. That's when I looked around and noticed Whites on one side of the street and Blacks on the other. I was a little scared at all this, so I crossed the street just to be safe.

When I arrived at the Savannah ballpark for our game my first night, I noticed the roped-off sections where the Blacks weren't allowed to enter. I couldn't believe it. I thought: *What the hell is going on?* And when they started coming into the ballpark, that's how it was. Segregation at the ballpark. And it made me angry. Later on, when we boarded the team bus for a road trip, the Black guys had to sit in the back of the bus. And when we stopped at some roadside truck stop to get some soda or a beer, the Black guys weren't allowed to go inside. We bought some sodas or some beer and would bring it back out to them on the bus.

My eventual Mets teammate was a Black player named Johnny Lewis. Lewis played for the Atlanta Crackers in 1963, when I played for Buffalo in the International League. We were playing against them in Atlanta for a series and you could hear them in the stands, heckling their own player with racial slurs. They'd yell out, "Hey Lewis, you're no Cracker. You're a Graham Cracker!"

They were terrible in the south back then and they got away with it. So many of these Black players had to go through things like this. And it happened all the time. Even later on in spring training, the Blacks weren't allowed to stay at the same hotel as we did. While us White players were right on a hotel beach in St. Petersburg enjoying the views and the nightlife, the Black players had to stay some place downtown. I don't recall where they stayed, but at 5:00 or 6:00 at night, they had to obey a curfew for all Blacks to stay off the beach area or get arrested. And there was nothing we could do about it.

It was scary, especially for someone like myself. Living in New York, we never had that kind of thing. You lived with them, you played with them. I had a lot of Black friends in the neighborhood, so this was quite an experience for me. I never knew what was going on in the beginning. So this was a lot to absorb early on. It wasn't just baseball lessons I was learning; it was cultural lessons as well.

The Mets called me back up with a little over two weeks to go in the season. And by then all the talk was about how bad they were and how close they'd gotten to the most losses in a single season since 1900. They'd hit the 110-loss mark and needed just eight more losses to become the record holder. Avoiding such a record would require winning eight of the last 14, and that seemed unlikely to me. A 17-game losing streak from May to June and an abysmal second half record had them chasing history. And I really thought I'd be playing by then, and what did they have to lose? Stengel kept me on the bench for another week, and by then the club lost another five games and trailed only the 1916 Philadelphia Athletics (117) for most losses in a season. The press had beaten the Mets up pretty good, and we'd become the laughingstock of the league. Jokes were being made about us—and probably for good reason.

It was just a few days before my high school graduation when Mets first baseman Marv Throneberry made his contribution to the Mets' woeful reputation as a bumbling, unfocused team with a base-running error I'd never seen or heard of before and haven't since. It's a story most Mets fans know, but it really defined that 1962 season quite well.

It was at the Polo Grounds when "Marvelous" Throneberry came up with two runners on base and hit a long drive into the gap. It was an easy triple that scored both runs, and Marvelous stood proudly at third, tipping his cap to the cheers of Mets fan.

While Throneberry was enjoying his moment, Chicago Cubs first baseman Ernie Banks was waving his arms and calling for the ball. When he got it, he stepped on the bag and said something to the umpire about Throneberry missing the bag. Without hesitation, the umpire signaled him out for missing the bag at first. Of course, Stengel came storming out of the dugout, but before he could say a word, the third-base umpire raised his hands and informed Stengel that Throneberry had also missed second base. It was stuff like this that followed the Mets all season long.

But I didn't find any of it funny. From the press to the mental mistakes to possibly being the team with the most losses in baseball history, I didn't want my name to be part of such a record. And I knew if I was in the lineup, I'd have that in the back of my mind and be bearing down even more than usual. Stengel told me two days before I was gonna start that he'd get me in for defense before that and he did. He got me into a couple games for defense late in the game, so you could imagine I didn't sleep those nights thinking about playing in my first game. When Stengel put me in as a defensive replacement for Hodges at first base, it was a bit of an odd feeling going in for him. I was half his age, and he was a legend with the Brooklyn Dodgers. But I didn't give it much thought. I handled myself well with three chances at first and later grounded out to second in my first major league at bat.

Hodges was great to me. He worked with me on footwork and positioning when he learned Stengel would be playing me, and in spring training the following season, he spent a lot of time with me, going over whatever situations there could be as a first baseman. Hodges was a very quiet individual, very sure of himself. He knew the game. You could tell he handled himself more maturely than the average baseball player and could see that military background coming through.

He wasn't a loud boisterous guy. He was very calm and collected and knew exactly what he was doing on the ball field. He was a different individual, in a good way. You could tell he was a student of the game, and he knew the game in every position, not just the perspective of a first baseman. He played the game the way it was supposed to be played, very professionally. Low key and no rah, rah, no jumping up and down after hitting a home run. He was a superstar in the league, one of the best power hitters of his time. He didn't throw the bat up in the air or jump around when he hit a home run. He just trotted around with a slow gait, went into the dugout, sat down. Didn't make a big deal out of it, didn't say much at all, if anything. I could tell right away that he'd make a good major league manager one day.

I don't know what the strategy was by Stengel, or why he chose to wait so long to play me. I figured you'd want to see your young players, and with the Mets' record and woes, this was his chance. When he started me the next day, I doubled off of Don Elston late in the game for my first major league hit. A single by Frank Thomas in the bottom of the ninth gave us the win and at least one more day of not tying the loss record by Philadelphia.

Nobody said a word to me when I came to the plate for my first major league at-bat. In the early days, we didn't have any of the closeness to the opposing players like they have today. You were on the other team, and that meant you were the enemy. You didn't talk to each other; that was the other team. We knew when Drysdale was going to retire because he came around the batting cages and nodded to you, acknowledging you with nothing more than that. But when he was pitching, he didn't talk to any of the opposing players because we were his enemy, and he was gonna knock you down. The only time we got together with any of the opposing players was at the All-Star Game, when we were teammates for a day, and the American League was the enemy. You had to talk in the dugout and the locker room to these guys, but when the game was over and we went back to the regular season, we were enemies again.

I didn't play at all at Milwaukee the next two games. We lost them both, and the record was ours. The next time I got in was the final game of the season as another defensive replacement for Throneberry at first. When I struck out looking in the ninth inning and Mantilla followed with a groundout for the final out of the season, the Mets' inaugural season was in the books. I tried to keep the good memories of the Mets' first season fresh in my mind, but there weren't very many. Even in our last game, we hit into a triple play.

The Mets won a doubleheader in May on walk-off home runs (we didn't call them that back then) by Hobie Landrith and Hodges. Thomas crushed 34 home runs, and Ashburn batted over .300 for the first time since he led the league in batting four years earlier. I guess you could call it grasping at straws, but that's what you need to do sometimes.

We didn't know it at the time, but Ashburn wasn't coming back for the '63 season. It came out later that he'd grown tired of all the losing, playing with 90-loss teams for the Phillies and Cubs before coming to the Mets in '62. Ashburn was a good guy and could still play and was our star player that year. I was only up for a short time, but he worked with the players and made a positive impression on me.

I'd only had a few weeks with the ballclub at the end of 1962, but Thomas told me a story involving himself, Ashburn, and shortstop Eli Chacon on a play that happened in the out-field. We all knew Chacon spoke hardly a word of English and somehow couldn't grasp when Ashburn yelled, "I got it!" on any fly ball that both guys might be going for. And because of that, they had a few collisions and a few balls dropped in for hits. Finally, Ashburn learned the Spanish phrase for I got it (*Yo la tengo*), and everything got better. Problem was they didn't let Thomas—who was our left fielder—in on it, and so he collided with Ashburn, who was our lone All-Star that year, one day when he heard him yell out, "*Yo la tengo!*"

Thomas said he got up and yelled out, "What the fuck is yellow tango?"

It wasn't just legendary players the Mets had on that '62 team. We also had Rogers Hornsby as our third-base coach and, supposedly, our hitting instructor. I was a student of the game and knew Hornsby had batted over .400 three times with big seasons of home runs and RBIs during his Hall of fame career. You read stories about his career and were in awe of what he did, but as good a hitter as he was, he was not an easy guy to deal with. If you asked for his help, he would tell you, "Just swing if it's a strike." Once when I was struggling, he said it again, then mumbled under this breath as he was walking away from me, "They don't make players like they used to."

You could tell he didn't want to be a hitting coach and didn't want to help the young players. His personality and reactions to the players on our team were entirely negative, and after a while, I found him to be insulting and worthless to me as a hitter, so I stayed away.

You can't process who you're playing with or being coached by as a 17 year old. So many of these guys were old Dodgers or from some other ballclub and past their primes. Some of these guys, like Hodges, were guys I followed when the Yankees played them in the World Series. It was crazy that these guys were now teammates of mine. What was even crazier was most guys my age were still in high school, hadn't even graduated yet, so I had to pinch myself every time I went to the ballpark thinking about that.

Chapter 4

CASEY AND THE CHARACTERS

THERE WAS STILL MORE BASEBALL for me to participate in following the end of the regular season, so the whirlwind tour of the country I'd experienced wasn't over yet. The New York Mets would be sending me down to the Florida Instructional League in St. Petersburg, where I'd meet up with all the other Mets prospects in the organization. I was looking forward to playing with guys my same age again, guys in the same boat as me. And I knew all eyes would be on me because of all then press I was getting.

The press made a big deal out of me signing with the Mets, and the Mets advertised me as the guy who could lead them out of the woodwork. I was gonna be this guy or that guy, a 30-homer, 100-RBI, .300-hitter for sure. I was headed for stardom like Al Kaline of the Detroit Tigers, a teenage phenom who'd become the star they'd hoped I'd become, and build the team around me and be just like the New York Yankees one day in the near future.

But I wasn't entirely sure I was quite ready to be that guy. I needed seasoning and had a taste of the competition and the pitching already in the minor leagues. As much as I wanted to be another Kaline, and as much as everybody wanted me to be, I knew it was going to be tough, but I was up for the challenge.

There weren't too many guys who became instant stars, especially against the likes of who was in the National League in '62. You look at baseball in the early '60s, and there were a lot of superstars and superstar pitchers. I'd already seen Sandy Koufax, Don Drysdale, Willie Mays, and Willie McCovey from the dugout, and the league was full of pitchers and other superstars like them or a notch below. And being just 17, it's tough to compare yourself to any players, let alone being the power hitting .300 hitter they'd predicted for me. On the pitching side of the game, I still hadn't seen Bob Gibson or Juan Marichal or Warren Spahn, and knew if I was to become a superstar, I'd have to get my baptism under fire.

In retrospect, I believe it was way too early for the majors, physically and mentally. And I'd found out soon enough that the mental part of baseball is as important as the physical part. Sure, I thought I had all the tools to become the superstar they were after, but living out of a suitcase wasn't easy. Traveling from city to city was at times tedious and boring. And if you count my high school and sandlot teams I played for that year, I played on six different clubs over five cities, not counting the upcoming Instructional League in Florida.

My first roommate with the Mets was Frank Thomas. He was a star with Pittsburgh and a star with the Mets in '62. But I was 17 and he was 33, double my age. I don't think I had anything in common with him. Don't get me wrong, Thomas was a great guy. He took me to his house in Pittsburgh once and introduced me to his family and gave me advice all the time about hitting. But I was too young to even go to the bars at nighttime with the guys, and this was when the legal age for drinking was 18. It was a great experience for me, but to play in the major leagues and have no friends on the road was tough, and projecting that to a full 162-game season and not the handful of games I spent with the team was on my mind a bit.

There were a lot of stories I'd heard about Thomas, about how strong he was. His hands were very strong, and he was very proud of it. Thomas had the strongest pair of hands I'd seen. That's why he was such a big home run hitter. He hit 34 home runs with the Mets that first year, so he was noted to be a strong guy.

And I remember him bragging that he could catch anybody's hardest throw from 90 feet away bare-handed! He would challenge guys from their other clubs and they put money on it. One day the San Francisco Giants came into the Polo Grounds and Mays—who had a pretty good arm and was a great player—came over to where Thomas was throwing, and Thomas challenged him. With that famous Willie Mays smile, Mays laughed and said confidently, "You can't catch my throw."

So everybody stopped what they were doing and Mays went about 90 feet from the plate, got a running start, and blazed one right at Thomas. Sure as shit, Thomas caught the ball and he didn't even flinch. All you could hear was it slap against his skin. I don't remember how much the bet was for, but he wanted his money on the spot. But Mays didn't pay him. For years, Thomas complained every time he saw Mays, "You never paid me!" But Mays never had any money on him and, as far as I know, hasn't paid him to this day.

That was fun watching those kinds of things, but I still was rooming with a guy twice my age. And I experienced it both ways by playing on the three minor league teams and the Mets that year. It was more fun for me rooming and playing with guys my own age in the minors. That's why I enjoyed the Florida Instructional League as much as I did and was where I first met Cleon Jones and all the other Mets prospects for the first time.

I could tell right away that Jones was the real thing. He was lightning fast and had good bat control. In one of our first games, he hit a routine grounder to the shortstop and still beat it out. But our manager, Solly Hemus, was good at pointing out all the negative things about us of us and called us over to him all the time. Hemus was another veteran guy like Casey Stengel and Rogers Hornsby, only much younger. He'd managed the St. Louis Cardinals for three years before coming over with the Mets and was a no-nonsense kind of guy. He had a chart and every day he wrote down how you fucked up, and at the top of that list were Ed Kranepool and Jones. After a while you start to question yourself, but in the end, I'm glad he did what he did. We both needed seasoning, and I guess Hemus could see we were the two best players in camp. Then, one day the Instructional League came to a halt, they cancelled the league and sent us home because of the Cuban Missile Crisis.

I never knew what a bubble I was living in until I signed my first contract. I'd seen the racism firsthand in Knoxville, Tennessee, but now the problems of the world had gone global, with Russia setting up nuclear armed missiles in Cuba—only 90 miles from the Florida coast. It was a tense time between Russia and the United States, so for our safety, they sent us home. The two countries finally came to some political agreement within a couple of weeks, but by that time, they weren't about to bring us back.

I never saw any rifts or fights between us in Florida, no problems between the races. Being that we were camped in the south, and from what I saw in Knoxville, I was on the lookout for anything out of the ordinary, or listening in on any racist comments. This was still the early '60s, and there were a lot of bigots and families still fighting the Civil War, and being from the North, that was one of my biggest surprises.

I had driven from New York to Florida in the first car I bought with my bonus—a brand new black top Ford Thunderbird. Originally, I came down to Florida by myself, but when we went home, I had my teammates and fellow New Yorkers, Larry Bearnarth and Mike Fiore, with me. I think Fiore slept the whole way back, and we were pissed at him for that. Bearnarth and I had to do all the driving, and Fiore was just one of those guys who had no problem sleeping in the car. I think the only time he woke up was when he was wet. We stopped for a bathroom break.

Bearnarth had been signed by the Mets, and we'd been team-mates for that short time I was in Syracuse, so we were familiar with each other. He was a right-handed pitcher who really struggled like I did in Syracuse. But he battled back and straightened himself out and made the Mets staff the following season. He bounced back and forth between the majors and the minors for years after that, finally calling it quits after 11 years and eight or nine teams. Later on, he became a minor league manager in the late '70s when I was still playing, so it was good to see he was still actively involved in the game.

Fiore was another guy the Mets signed in the amateur draft. He never made the Mets roster, but it sure wasn't for lack of trying. Fiore plugged along in the minors for years and finally made it to the big leagues in 1968. He was another guy who kept himself in the game, going from city to city and league to league, hoping to make it and stay on a major league roster. I took a look and counted the teams he played on, and it was a mind-boggling 18 teams in 16 seasons. I thought the five teams I'd played on in 1962 was unusual, and I guess it was, but this was ridiculous. And you have to give him credit for staying the course.

Even on graduation day after I signed my Mets contract, there was no time for a neighborhood celebration or even a graduation party. I was out the door in two days. And some of my friends had gone off to college, and a few had come back for the summer. After talking with some of them about the college experience, I knew it would have been great for me, especially the camaraderie that college sports brought out.

But I didn't wish I'd gone to college instead of going right into baseball. My life's thoughts and dreams were always to play baseball. I ended up having a great life doing that. I played 18 years, played in a tough city—New York—and playing in your home city is probably the toughest thing to do. If you speak to any athlete who plays at home and in particular New York because of all the writers and national attention you'd get, he or she would tell you it was hard. People are always critiquing how you played and remembering you as a star. I was always the star growing up and I found out soon enough your star gets tarnished when you're on a bad team and you're not hitting .300.

The Mets organization, undoubtedly, force-fed me to the major leagues. They wanted to send me to the minor leagues after the first year of spring training, but Stengel had a limited roster with a lot of older players at the twilight of their careers.

The Mets general manager was George Weiss, the old executive of the Yankees, and he was adamant about sending me to the minor leagues during spring training in '63. But Stengel convinced Weiss to see how I performed in a couple of games in spring training and then evaluate me afterward. Stengel put me into the lineup, and as it ended up, I led the club in hitting. So Stengel goes to Weiss and asked, "How can I send him out? He's my best player?" Then right after that, when we came north on the last weekend of spring training, I hit three home runs in a game against the Baltimore Orioles. Stengel made his point again to Weiss, stating things like, "There's no way I'm sending him out. He might be a surprise player." So I opened the regular season in right field batting third.

Earlier in the spring, Stengel put me in right and told me I was gonna be his right fielder. He went around to all the positions and talked to each player about his position and gave little bits of advice I'd never heard before. I think he spent more time with me in right field than he normally would have, but he wanted me to be as ready as I could be for Opening Day. Stengel wanted me in right because we already had two first baseman, Gil Hodges and Marv Throneberry. Stengel came over to right and told me he wanted to see my arm and to throw to all the bases. "I'm gonna show you how to throw from the outfield," I remember him saying to me.

So I threw a ball to second and then another one to third, neither one on a straight line like Roberto Clemente or one of those other great right fielders in the league. Now, I knew I didn't have a strong arm and always thought I had more of an infielder's arm, but I threw the ball as hard and as straight as I could, but it still had that little loop to it. Stengel saw the loop and said angrily, "Give me the ball." Stengel took the ball and as he wound up to throw to third base, he threw the ball right into the ground and almost hit himself in the foot. He said, "That's the way I want you to throw. Keep the ball low!" I wanted to laugh, but that wouldn't be a good idea around Stengel. He was a showman, that's for sure, and I didn't know what he would have thought if some 18-year-old soft throwing player like myself started laughing. But he always made his point just like he did that day.

We opened the 1963 season at the Polo Grounds against the Cardinals, a shutout loss to Ernie Broglio. I flied out three times and saw the ball pretty good, but if it hadn't been for Larry Burright's two hits, we would have opened the year with a no-hitter tossed against us.

The Cardinals had a deep lineup at just about every position, and, of course, the biggest name was Stan Musial. Musial was 42 and still producing numbers you wouldn't expect from guys that age. He was coming off a year in which he batted .330, made the All-Star team for a 17th straight season, and didn't look to me as if he was slowing down. By season's end, that was it for him, so I was grateful I got to play against him and see him perform up close. With all the expectations they had for me, I could only hope I'd become half the player he was.

Our lineup was nothing like the Cardinals. Aside from myself in right, we had an old outfield with Thomas and Duke Snider and a collection of weak singles hitters around the infield. As I looked around our infield, I didn't understand why the Mets had traded Felix Mantilla in the off-season for Al Moran. Mantilla was one of the bright spots on that '62 team, and that was it. One and done. It was probably the first time I'd questioned a management decision, at least to myself, but I was too young and too inexperienced to talk about it with anybody.

I didn't like playing in the Polo Grounds because it was such an odd-shaped field. When I played left field, you'd back up on a fly ball, and the ball would land in the upper deck for a home run. You wouldn't even see the baseball because the lower level was 20 feet farther back, so you'd be thinking you had a beat on the ball for an easy catch, and instead it was a cheap home run.

It was a tough field to hit in because I wasn't strong enough yet to pull the ball down the right-field line, and the pitchers were smart enough to keep the ball on the outside part of the plate. If you tried to pull the ball on a pitch like that, it would end up in no-man's land out in right center or center field where it was anywhere from 430' to 480'. It was such a big place that when the attendance was just a few thousand, you could hear what some fans were saying. It was easy to hear a guy yelling at you and as the season progressed it was at times depressing playing in a stadium that was old and in disarray, with older players playing out their career. Later in the year, we played the last game at the Polo Grounds in September in front of a really small crowd. I don't have any real memories of that game, only that I didn't play. All I know is we were anxious to move in to brand new Shea Stadium in '64.

I got off to a good start and was hitting .300 at the end of April. But my production—if you call it that—was off the charts bad. Two RBIs for the entire month of April wasn't what they'd expected from a middle of the lineup hitter, but it seemed like hardly anyone was ever in scoring position when I came to bat. We had a nice little four-game winning streak in April, then it was all downhill from there for both the team and for myself. By the end of May, I hit a big slump and by early July I dipped below .200. That's when they sent me back to Triple A Buffalo. Stengel called me into his office and said we're gonna send you to Buffalo to get some work down there, and the next thing you know I looked around and said, "Wait a second. What about my bonus?"

I was aware I had a bonus coming up had I stayed on the major league roster for 90 days, and this was day 88. When I first signed a contract, everybody in baseball had a special clause in their contract that stipulated you had to be on the roster for 90 consecutive days to earn part of your bonus, and mine was $7,500. Weiss was shrewd and decided to send me down at the All-Star break, just a couple of days before my bonus went into effect.

So I told all this to Stengel and I was upset and said they couldn't do that to me. I had my progressive bonus coming. Stengel was surprised and obviously didn't know anything about it because he wasn't aware of the fine details in any of our contracts. I asked Stengel if he could get Weiss to wait just a few more days so I could get my bonus, a figure that basically amounted to my annual salary. Once he understood, he called Weiss, and Weiss told Stengel what I said was true. Stengel didn't ask but told him not to send me out until after the All-Star break. I had a little leverage with the ballclub because of the bonus I had signed with them, so they agreed with Stengel and kept me around for a few more days. But that's how Stengel was for his players. He'd battle for you and protect you and take all the heat from the press when he had to.

They had two other guys in that situation, and Grover Powell was one of them. He ended up a few days short, so he didn't make the progressive bonus. Next spring, he showed up and hurt his arm and got sent to the minor leagues, never to be heard from again. That's the way they did it back then. They'd do what they could to curtail money.

They had a lot of old-time guys in Buffalo, like Dick Ricketts and our manager, Kerby Farrell. Earlier in the year, the Mets had demoted Throneberry—the same guy who had the base running gaffe in '62 when he missed two bases on the same hit. Throneberry was a great guy with a Mickey Mantle-type swing, and everybody thought he was gonna be a great player because of his credentials in the minor leagues in Denver. Throneberry had a three-year stretch where he averaged close to 40 home runs a season and 130 RBIs but struggled up top. He was a great player, and the Yankees thought they had something special, but he never had a chance to play over there with the Yankees. But he had a great swing. He idolized Mantle and everything he did was copied from Mantle.

And Throneberry really struggled with Buffalo after the Mets sent him down. He had his share of home runs, but his average hovered around .180. The Mets never called him back up, and he'd be done playing altogether within a year. That's something I didn't dwell on back then. I was 18 and had my whole career in front of me. But I'd already been on the yo-yo between the major and the minors and could see lots of veteran guys on the bubble like Throneberry and didn't want one of those guys to be me.

Buffalo has rainy, snowy, shitty weather, and this is true even into May. So when I was down there, that caused a lot of makeup games to be played as doubleheaders late in the year, and that's what we were facing down the stretch. I think we had five doubleheaders in seven days, but we didn't have 25 or 30 players like you did in the major leagues. You had only 21 players on the entire roster. Of course, that really depletes your pitching staff, so it was impossible to have enough pitching to win.

Some of those teams had amazing pitching staffs, which made for good competition. Jacksonville alone had Tommy John, Sam McDowell, Mike Cuellar, and Sonny Siebert—all guys that became stars in the American League. And Jacksonville had the worst record in the league.

Anyway, we were still in contention facing all these doubleheaders, then, shit, you'd lose a doubleheader, then you'd come back the next day and win one out of two, and then lose another doubleheader. But the game that cost us a shot at the championship in the middle of all those doubleheaders was on an error by none other than "Marvelous" Throneberry at first base.

When Throneberry was with the Mets, he had articles written about him making running mistakes or fielding mistakes, things like that, so it would come as no surprise to anyone that he missed a routine ground ball in such an important game. We got into the clubhouse, Farrell locked the door to his office, and one of the guys noticed he was crying. Throneberry noticed himself and yelled out, "I've played lots of baseball over my career, but this is the first time a manager cried over me." The whole club was really laughing hard at that one.

The 1963 year turned out to be quite an interesting one. Just before we broke camp from spring training, the Mets acquired another Old Dodger, Snider, from the Dodgers. Ever since the Dodgers left Brooklyn, his playing time had steadily gone down, but he was still a good hitter despite being 36 years of age. His power numbers had dropped off, but he was still one of the top home run hitters of all time. Teaming him up with Hodges again certainly would have some interest from our old Dodgers fans, but they were both well past their primes. The two of them got into the same starting lineup only once and played in a few other games together but only that once as starters. By the end of May, the Mets decided to trade him to the Washington Senators for an unusual guy named Jimmy Piersall.

Piersall had been known to be a flaky guy. He did some odd stuff like wear a Little League helmet to a game, throw a ball at the scoreboard, and run around the outfield trying to distract Ted Williams at the plate. He had some fights and multiple ejections and he'd been hospitalized and underwent electric shock therapy to try to calm him down. But he was a talented player, and the Mets seemed to be willing to try anything back then.

Stengel put him into center field and had him leading off, but I knew that wouldn't last. I'd never seen so many lineups, especially guys leading off, and this was only May. By season's end, Stengel had about 20 guys batting leadoff, including myself for a bunch of games at the end. You never knew with Stengel what he was going to do with the lineup. He would put whoever he thought to lead off, especially if the club was losing, and we lost all the time. He'd pull them out of a hat sometimes. He did all kinds of things. And he batted me second a few times, and that's when I learned how to sacrifice bunt because that was a big part of his game. With him, anything could happen. He wasn't gonna get criticized, so he didn't care. I didn't like batting first or second. I had always batted in the middle of the lineup, but I never said anything because I just wanted to play.

Like so many others who came to the Mets, Piersall struggled to stay above .200. And remember, if there was a comedian on the field, it was going to be Stengel. He didn't want any competition for that role because he savored it. And on the occasion of Piersall hitting his 100th career home run, his antics that followed got him an early exit as a Met. But we found out later that Piersall was upset at the way Snider's 400th career home run was handled when he hit it about 10 days earlier, and he was not trying to draw attention to himself.

I guess Piersall had a good point because only six other guys in the history of the game had reached 400 career home runs, and three of them were still playing. Later in the season, Mays would join Eddie Mathews, Mantle, and Snider in that special circle of sluggers, so it really was a big deal. As much as I respected Snider, I had an incident with him earlier in the year when I was taking batting practice at the Polo Grounds. I'd mentioned I started the season in right field and was doing fairly well but was tailing off as of late. I was trying too hard to pull the ball to take advantage of the short porch down the line at the Polo Grounds, but it wasn't working.

So Stengel brought me to the plate and said, "Ed, you've been pulling the ball too much. I'm gonna send out Hemus and Kress to pitch extra batting practice to you and I'm gonna sit in my office and watch the whole thing."

He called Hemus over and told him to pitch them all over the place, and that he was looking for me to hit everything to the left of second base. Stengel looks at me with a stern look on his face and said, "If I see you pull the ball to right field, even one time, I'm gonna send you down to Triple A tomorrow." And with that, he headed for his office in straightaway center field.

So I'm standing in the batter's box knowing Stengel's watching me with his binoculars and knowing I have to take every pitch to left, regardless if it's a sweet one on the inside part of the plate. Then out of the clubhouse walks Snider.

Snider went behind the cage to watch me hit and after a while he began to notice I'm not pulling the inside pitches into right field. He was getting mad as he saw me continuing to hit balls to the left side and finally said to me, "What are you doing? Pull the ball into right field. What are you doing?"

But, I was paying no attention to what he had to say. I was thinking in the back of my mind that Stengel's watching me in center field, so I didn't give a shit what kind of swing I was taking. I was just following his instructions.

Snider was getting angry, and he said it a little stronger, "Ed, what the hell's wrong with you? Pull that ball!" And he was right. But meanwhile, I was in my own head knowing Stengel's watching me and if I hit just one ball to the right of second, he's gonna send me to the minor leagues. So I didn't give a shit what Snider said. I was paying attention to what Stengel told me. So Snider says, "Goddamn it, pull the ball to right you big ass hole." So I turned around and said, "Shut the fuck up, Duke. You're not doing too good yourself."

Well, one of the writers happened to be there when I blasted Snider and saw the whole thing. And when I finished batting practice, Snider walks away pissed that some 18-year-old kid is telling a great player what to do. But meanwhile he didn't know the situation, and maybe I should have said something when he started barking instructions at me. But I was concentrating so hard at not pulling the ball, so I didn't say a word about it.

Snider walked away, and he's angry, and the writer knew he had a scoop. He told all the other writers and wrote the story about the Mets brash rookie Ed Kranepool blasting Duke Snider. I should have never said that to him, but it was the heat of the moment kind of thing. I should have respected him, so I apologized to Snider later and I told him exactly what was going on with Stengel. He said, "Oh, I understand now why you were doing everything wrong," and I apologized again and we got along fine after that—only the writers didn't follow up and write that part to the story. They'd rather just tell the part of the story that sells copies, I guess. The press got all over me about it for a while, and I got along great with Snider after that. We had no hard feelings, but that story travelled around, and nobody forget about it for a couple of years.

Stengel didn't say anything to the writers about it because there was so much negative publicity going on. But Stengel stood up for the players anytime you played for him. If you put out and played hard for him, he would protect you. But he didn't say anything then.

Chapter 5

SPITTERS, SPOILERS, AND 100 MORE LOSSES

THE NEW YORK METS HELD A team dinner every year around the second week of spring training that was hosted by our owner, Mrs. Joan Payson. She didn't cut back on anything. Steaks, lobster, booze. You name it. I'd gotten along with her since the day we met. And in later years, I think it's part of the reason the Mets never traded me.

Mrs. Payson loved the Giants and always wanted to bring baseball back to New York when they left for San Francisco. She was like a grandmother to the players, a really wonderful person. She sat next to our dugout and came to the games with her family, said hello to everybody, and was a fan. She always did something nice for the players. If there was a new baby in your family, she'd send you a gift and sent gifts on other occasions. She'd just be sweet all the time and never interfered with the game. She was a real fan, and that's the way it was with her.

It was Casey Stengel's job to say a few words about the ballclub, but usually he was long-winded and would ramble on with one story, which led to another and then another. Stengel got up to make a speech and he started rambling like he always did, and it was long and very entertaining, but what he was saying wasn't making a lot of sense. After a while, people were getting restless, moving around and fidgeting and waiting for him to get done talking. That's when Duke Carmel decided to make a funny comment, hoping he's gonna get a few laughs out of it.

But just like with Rod Kanehl and Jimmy Piersall, Stengel didn't think it was funny and started blasting Carmel about his abilities as a player and reminding him he hadn't made the ballclub yet. Then Stengel took it even further, saying stuff about Carmel that he caught him at such-and-such a place and out at nighttime past curfew. He really ripped him, and it was the second time I saw Stengel go crazy, the Piersall incident being the first time. Finally, Stengel settled down, but the next thing you know, Carmel was sent to the minors where he had a great year but never made it back to the Mets.

I wasn't surprised that Stengel knew about Carmel's after-game hangouts because he knew all of them on every player. He was cunning in how he came to know how he caught everybody at night. Stengel was a heavy smoker and every time he caught you doing something, he'd say, "Hey, give me a pack of matches." I didn't smoke, so he never asked me, but the guys that did were usually in for a rude awakening.

Suppose we were in St. Louis and Stengel got a pack of matches from a player. All the bars and restaurants had their name on the cover, and Stengel would collect them, then at a team meeting he might say something like, "Carmel, you were at such-and-such a club," so he'd bring it up, and the guys had no idea at first how he knew.

He was smart. He caught a lot of guys at that shit. Finally, they figured it out, but he knew the hangouts of all of us. And he always sat at the bar in the hotels right near the door. He was the first one there at night and the last to leave, and the bar was off limits to the players. He'd sit there and close the bar every night, but if you came in, he could see the door and would catch you. That's how he caught a lot of guys after curfew. He had the press all in the bar and he always picked up the tab. The press was so cheap they'd rather be with Stengel and drink with him all night. Plus, you never knew with Stengel what story you're gonna get. It could be from 50 years ago and it could be from 50 minutes ago. He would start on a story and go on a ramble, and you had no idea sometimes where he was going with it, but he'd get a flashback and start talking about one player then went into another player, stuff like that. Stengel was usually a fun-loving guy, but he wanted the last word on everything.

I was still just 19 on Opening Day in 1964, and I was determined to stay on the club the whole year. But I hadn't heard the end of the comparisons yet and probably for good reason, I'd had 300 at-bats in the majors but was under .200 with hardly any run production or power. Meanwhile, out in Detroit, Al Kaline had made another All-Star team, so the comparisons kept coming. And even though Kaline had blossomed into a superstar, he didn't show any power until he turned 20. Plus, he had guys like Norm Cash and Rocky Colavito around him in the lineup.

It didn't help to see a banner on Opening Day that read, "Is Ed Kranepool over the hill?" I mean, come on. What kind of fans writes that kind of stuff? I heard about another sign at Wrigley Field on Opening Day once that said, "Wait til' next year." I never found that sort of thing to be funny and never liked that Sign Man guy at Shea because of it. I thought he was the biggest asshole in baseball, always holding up a sign that read, "Big Stiff" when I came to bat. If I stood over your desk while you're working and critiqued everything you do—both good and bad—how would you react to that? You wouldn't like it or stand for it for very long. But what could I do about it? Not much.

But I was seething inside when I kept seeing those negative signs. Even when I didn't look over to where he set up, I knew what was going on. He wasn't a creative person and he wasn't a fan because a fan roots for the guys in good times and bad. You've got to encourage the players—especially the young guys coming up—and can't just be critiquing guys and making fun of people when they do something wrong. Nobody wanted to make an error and nobody wanted to strike out at the wrong time. I've never met a player who wants to look bad before 50,000 people.

In later years, he wanted to come back on the plane with us, but we didn't want him there. I never did want to talk with him and encountered him once. He may have apologized for being so hard on me, but I wasn't ready to become his friend or forget about any of it. Some of the players may have been amused by him, but I never appreciated his negative signs riling up the fans. Sometimes it's hard to get the fans back on your side when that happens. He was nothing but a negative person, and I didn't think what he did was funny. But it burns you internally with what this guy had to say. I certainly didn't go out of my way to rip him in the newspapers because you can't win those battles.

So I wanted to get off to a good start in a new ballpark and make the Sign Guy eat his words, but that didn't happen. I didn't play very much in April, mostly used as a pinch-hitter, and never even played in a game that we'd won. By mid-May they'd seen enough of my .139 batting average, one extra-base hit, and not a single RBI. So, as was the norm for me, they shuffled me off to Buffalo again to get some consistent playing time and, hopefully, my swing back.

Granted, I wasn't playing every day, but then I was already pressing and looking over my shoulder to being sent down, and that's when it happened. I was tired of the going back and forth between cities, but I understood. I also understood that the pitchers were very smart. Whatever they lacked in speed, they'd make up with deception and craftiness, cunning ways they'd learned to get you out. They'd learned what your strengths and weaknesses were and learned to work around you. That's when inexperience takes over. I wanted to swing. I didn't want to walk. I wanted to hit. And when you're aggressive, sometimes you get yourself out by swinging at the wrong pitches. The saying about the sophomore slump was really all about pitchers making better adjustments than the hitters. They figured you out. They did what they had to do to get you out, and if you still struggled, you got sent out.

I was just an aggressive, fastball hitter, and being young, I had good reflexes and could catch up to most fastballs. A lot of times if a pitch looked good it might be a little bit out of the strike zone, and that's what they'd do to entice a hitter—especially at the Polo Grounds. The next thing I knew, I was changing my approach or trying a different swing and confused as hell about all of it. But it was all on me, and that's when I really struggled because I had no coach or film to help me.

I was excited to leave the Polo Grounds for Shea Stadium until I saw what the ground crew did with the infield. They'd grow the grass extra thick and water it down before the games to help the pitching staff more than the hitter. By game time, the grass was still pretty damp, and when the ball hit on the grass part, it slowed right down to a crawl, even the hard-hit grounders. It may have been good for any ground-ball pitcher, but not for line-drive hitting guys like me with not much speed. Sure, it bothers you as a hitter because you'd take a beating with your average so many times when you thought you had a hit. Later on, when all the turf fields were built, I loved to play on those because balls that would have been outs at Shea were going through, sometimes even to the wall.

I know when my career ended I had good averages at all the turf stadiums, except the Astrodome and the few games we played at Olympic Stadium. But I was well over .300 in Cincinnati, St. Louis, Pittsburgh, and Philadelphia, where I took advantage of those fields. I sometimes wonder what I would have done if Shea had been on a turf field or had regular grass that wasn't so thick. I think things would have been a lot different for me, a lot better, in fact. Probably would have hit .300 or close to it.

I did quite well in Buffalo for two weeks. I was playing every day and batted over .300 with a few home runs. But after playing both ends of a doubleheader on May 30th, I got the call to rejoin the Mets in New York for a scheduled doubleheader against the Giants. I caught an early morning flight from Syracuse to Newark, hopped a cab to Shea Stadium, and suited up.

I wasn't sure what Stengel was planning to do with me. In the few games I'd played with the Mets, it was mostly in the outfield, but I'd played all 15 games with Buffalo at first base, taking over for Carmel, who they promptly shifted to the outfield when I arrived. I was more comfortable at first base than the outfield, but I didn't care where they used me. I just wanted to play. And the Mets had Tim Harkness at first base, but because of a slump similar to the one I had before I was demoted, he was benched right after I left for Buffalo. Harkness was hitting close to .400 by the end of April until it all went downhill after that. That prolonged slump gave Dick Smith an opening to be the everyday first baseman in Stengel's revolving door of players, and that's where Stengel put him during those few weeks in late May.

But Smith was no power hitter or run producer, and the league was full of them at first base. With guys like Ernie Banks, Bill White, Deron Johnson, and Orlando Cepeda, this was the type of stability with power hitters the Mets were after, what they'd wanted all along, and what they were sorely lacking in. But I wasn't giving much thought to the league in general, just to my situation. I could see this as another opportunity to play at first base and to play every day. The fact that they'd shifted Carmel to the outfield in Buffalo and benched Harkness were good signs for me. But I knew I had to perform. Every ball player knows that. You don't stay around for very long batting under .200 in the major leagues, even on a team like the Mets. I knew I had to take advantage of the situation and was hoping Stengel would play me right away. And he did. I started at first base and batted sixth for the first game of the doubleheader and went 1–4 off of Juan Marichal. We had them early but couldn't hold a 3–0 lead and lost 5–3.

Stengel came right over to me after the game and asked me if I was good to go again, that the team was kind of short on players. He said he'd take me out at some point in the game, but he also knew I was young and had a lot of energy. And I knew I could do it. I'd played five games in one day at times back on the sandlot, and it wasn't as if I'd be running all over the field playing at first base. So Stengel kept me at first and moved me up to fifth in the lineup.

You never know in baseball what you might see or what kind of strange play might happen during a game. I'd already witnessed a no-hitter on my first day in the majors, a triple play, and had been there for Piersall's running the bases backward, any number of things. It may be a long season playing on a losing team, but along the way, unforgettable things happen.

That second game started out like most games, playing from behind. After trailing 6–1 after five innings, it looked to be a sure sweep by the Giants, much to the delight of the thousands of Giants fans that packed the stadium. Attendance was over 57,000 and usually was a sellout when we played the Giants or the Los Angeles Dodgers. It seemed like half our yearly attendance came from those games. It was tremendous to be playing in front of such a big crowd. And when we rallied in the sixth and tied it in the seventh, our fans were going crazy.

I singled with two out in the ninth but was left stranded. To that point I'd gone 3-of-5, just a home run shy of hitting for the cycle and was feeling pretty good about myself. I saw a good pitch from Bobby Bolin on my first at bat and hit it hard but right at Willie Mays in center for an out, then grounded to first in my second at-bat. I was thinking to myself, *Here we go again* when I came up again in the sixth. But I tripled that scored a run, doubled my next at-bat, and had that infield single in the ninth. We could have won the game right there but ended up going into extra innings tied 6–6.

Hitting for the cycle may have been in the back of my mind, but I batted in the ninth and wasn't due up for at least another few innings, and by that time, there was a chance the game would be over. I got my chance in the 12th but struck out, then again in the 14th. We traded zeros for another eight innings before the Giants won it in the 23rd on a double by Del Crandall, who was pinch hitting for Gaylord Perry.

Perry had come into the game in the 13th and ended up pitching 10 innings of scoreless relief and ended up with the win. That may have been one of the story lines of the game, but I considered mine to be more unique. By the time that second game had ended, I had played four games within a span of 24 hours, with that 23-inning game ending about 10 minutes till 12. My comments afterward to the press were that I wished we had played 10 more minutes because I may have been the only player to have started a game in May and ended it in June.

You saw guys out there that looked bowlegged when they took the field. They didn't allow us to have any solid food during doubleheaders for some reason, so they gave us a cup of soup and crackers, and that was it. But it wasn't enough to sustain most guys. We'd arrive at the ballpark after having breakfast at around 10 AM, so it had been about 14 hours since we'd had a decent meal. That's a long time considering all the energy that had been expended, and it showed on the field. Guys were worn out. But guys were really tough back then. Both—Tom Haller for the Giants and our own Chris Cannizzaro—caught the entire game, which basically amounted to a tripleheader. Guys played out of their normal positions. Even Mays played shortstop for a while. It was crazy to see.

Before that doubleheader, Perry had started a week earlier against Pittsburgh and was shelled. But he'd also picked up a win, including the win by pitching the last inning of another 15-inning marathon game a few weeks earlier. He'd appeared in only a few games thus far, and while he struggled with the other teams, he really seemed to have our number.

I'm sure that at some point in the 23-inning game, Perry began throwing spitballs for the first time. He looked to be the odd man out with the Giants and, in all likelihood, on his way down to the minors, so he started throwing balls with all kinds of shit on it. I'd faced him before, but suddenly his pitches had so much more movement on it. Pitches looked good but suddenly were dropping in the dirt at the last moment. You'd pick up a ball with some shiny dirt or greasy texture and hand it to the umpire, but they were so tired they didn't care about any of that stuff. So he got away with it. He put Vaseline every-where after that game. On the brim of his cap, on the back of his thumb. He got really good at hiding it from the umpires. He developed different ways of pitching. Before he started dabbling in all this, he was a fastball, curveball-type pitcher, then added all the gyrations to try to confuse the hitter. He threw hard and was a nice guy to hit against with nothing exceptional, a mediocre pitcher at best. But look what he went on to do after that. By reinventing himself, he became a 20-game winner mul-tiple times, won over 300 games in his career, and was inducted into the Hall of Fame.

All this was confirmed by his teammate Bob Shaw when we acquired him from the Giants a year later. Shaw's the guy who taught Gaylord how to doctor up the ball and how to hide it from the umpires. And because he was so good at it himself, part of the reason why we lost Roy McMillan to an injury was due in part to that spitter he threw. After one of Shaw's spit-ters, McMillan took a grounder at short, and the ball didn't feel right to him when he began his throw to first. So he hung onto the ball at the last second and he hurt his shoulder when he decided not to release it. He had another injury with a fan later on, went through a rehab, but that was it for him.

Following that doubleheader, I started playing every day and had a 13-game hitting streak, in which I batted over .340, raising my average to over .260. And I was knocking in some runs, finally hitting a home in a win against the Dodgers. When they traded Harkness in late July, I knew the job was mine. Now I just had to keep it. But I hit a slump for a few weeks, then got hot again, getting close to .280 in early August. I sort of was up and down for the duration of the season, and going into the final series of the year in St. Louis, I was sitting on nine home runs and really wanted to end up in double figures for the season.

We hadn't played any meaningful games all year and hadn't played any at all during my short time with the club. As a player who'd been used to being in the championship series all his life, that took some getting used to and wasn't a good feeling to have.

But we'd played better ball in the second half and had won nine of 11 in August that almost gave us our first winning month as a franchise. I'd put together another decent hitting streak of seven games during that stretch, but more importantly was contributing by knocking guys in, collecting several RBIs and doing it when it mattered. I singled in the home half of the 10th to beat the Chicago Cubs 2–1 and had a single and a sacrifice fly in our 3–1 win over the Cincinnati Reds. It's one thing to win, but being a contributor to those wins was a big ego boost.

I tried to dwell on what we'd done lately instead of checking out the league standings, but we knew where we stood. Dead last by a mile. And checking the rest of the league, it looked like a sure bet that the Philadelphia Phillies were going to the World Series. With about 40 games to go in the season, there was still time for the Reds or Giants to catch up—or even the St. Louis Cardinals who sat a full nine games back. The Phils had made their move right around the same time we got hot in August. They'd taken six straight from us over a week's period before we finally beat them. But they'd gone from being a game ahead to seven games up in about three weeks of games and still led by six with about two weeks to go. That's when the unthinkable happened to them.

We were excited that we could be the spoiler for someone's party. And it felt good playing in meaningful games for once. It felt so much better than playing out the string against some other club that had been eliminated from contention. We still had five left with the Reds and three with the Cardinals, so we had a role to play. The Reds had just swept the Phils before they came into Shea for five games, cutting the Phils' lead to three-and-half games. While the Phillies lost four more home games to the Milwaukee Braves, the Reds pitching dominated us, giving up just four runs in the five-game sweep. And in what seemed to be an instant, the Reds passed Philadelphia in the standings with St. Louis right behind. But the Cardinals swept Philadelphia at home, the Phillies 10th loss in a row, and with the Reds taking just one of three from the Pirates, it had come down to the Cardinals, Reds, and Phillies for the pennant.

There'd been much criticism given to Phillies manager Gene Mauch for the way he handled his pitching during that unbelievable collapse at the end, and deservedly so. He used Jim Bunning and Chris Short on short rest, sending both guys out there in six of those 10 losses. That was surprising to us because he had Art Mahaffey and he'd lost a tough, 1–0 game to the Reds that started their losing streak. Then Short got roughed up by the Reds, Dennis Bennett followed with a loss, and then it was Bunning's turn to lose. Mahaffey started one more time, but from there it was mostly Bunning and Short.

I wasn't fond of those moves by Mauch. That would bring out some animosity in a player, you would think. I know I would have been upset if something like that would have happened to me with the manager having no confidence in you all of a sudden. I didn't think Philadelphia deserved to win because of poor managing. I'd find out all about the importance of a manager in situations that decide a pennant later on in 1973. But for now, we still could play the role of spoiler. We went into St. Louis on the last weekend of the season with a more serious disposition than we had in the game we played there earlier in the season, and that had everything to do with Stengel.

With Stengel, you never knew what was gonna come out of his mouth. He loved the press and he loved to talk to them. We were in St. Louis earlier in the year, and the Cardinals were beating on us pretty good when they loaded the bases. Stengel came out to change pitchers, and he was taking his time, and you could tell he knew he was annoying the umpires. He got to the mound and he was thinking about what he should do, but he already knew what he was gonna do. The umpire had enough and he came over to the mound and said rather firmly, "Stengel, make a decision on this pitcher." Stengel looked down to the bullpen and raised both of his hands, but his left hand went up a split second before his right hand did, so Barlick called in the left-handed pitcher, and Stengel threw up his hands again, only this time he was pissed at Barlick.

Everybody knew it wasn't a smart baseball move, bringing in the righty to face Ken Boyer, Mike Shannon, or whatever right-handed batter it was. Anyhow, whichever player it was, he was standing at the plate smiling like he knew it was a mistake before he hit the ball hard right at our shortstop, and we get out of the inning. Now everybody's excited in the dugout because Stengel looked like a genius, and he was gloating and happy as a pig in shit.

The next day the managers met at home plate to exchange lineup cards, and after Stengel got back to the dugout, the plate umpire got my attention and asked that Stengel come back out to the plate. I turned around and waved at Stengel, and he ran halfway up to the plate and he said, "What's wrong? You got a problem today?"

So the ump said, "Well, you have only eight names on your lineup. You forgot the pitcher."

Stengel said, "You did such a good job picking them yester-day. Pick them today!" Now everybody's laughing, including the umpire.

But now this was a serious time, and we were hoping to spoil the Cardinals' party. It wasn't as if we were rooting for the Reds or the Phillies to win the pennant because we didn't care at all who won it. We just wanted to win and give them something positive to say or write about us. And the Cardinals had really taken us for granted when we came in. To save money on travel expenses, the Mets decided to keep half the roster at home. Rosters had been expanded, but we may have had 20 guys total to make the trip. And the Cardinals were hot and had something more to play for than we did.

With champagne on ice, we surprised them and won the opener, a 1–0 shutout over Gibson, courtesy of my single in the fourth that brought in the only run of the game. Then we pounded 20-game winner Ray Sadecki the next day, knock-ing him out after just an inning and continuing the barrage against their bullpen. I contributed again with four RBIs and my 10th home run of the year off of my old teammate Roger Craig. We won easily 15–5. With the Reds and Phillies off that day, the Cardinals and Reds were tied, and the Phillies trailed by a game. It was simple math for the Cardinals. A win and a Reds loss would give them the pennant. A win and a Reds win would create a two-way tie. A loss and a Reds win would give the Reds the pennant, or a loss and a Phils win would create a three-way tie.

We'd really surprised them by winning those first two games and we were confident we'd get the sweep and we actually were ahead 3–2 in the fifth. With the Cardinals keeping one eye on the scoreboard from Cincinnati, the Cardinals scored three times in the fifth, sixth and eighth innings to put the game away, clinching the division with the Reds losing 10–0.

That was the most fun we'd had all year, and I put it in the back of my mind that no lead is ever safe, even being seven games up like Philadelphia was with 10 to play. It was a grind, an every-day grind. And teams like St. Louis and Cincinnati had proven how it could be done, how to chip away and that you never give up. So I took that mindset to the off-season, thinking about our future and being in a pennant race from start to finish. It was a good exercise for the mind and the soul, but I knew we were a far cry from the talent level of those three teams. We had a long way to go.

And so did I. Everybody knew that 10 home runs weren't a number they'd expected of me by now, but I was progressing and still only 19 years of age. Maybe they could finally see for themselves I was more of a line-drive hitter that was looking to drive the ball and not go for home runs. Maybe I'd become that 20-home run guy and not the 30-home run guy they thought they were getting.

But we weren't a power-hitting club and hadn't built a lineup with power-hitting guys. We had only one guy hitting 20, and that was Charley Smith. That was one of the few good deals the Mets had pulled off when they acquired Smith from the Chicago White Sox, and maybe the club was finally going to have some stability at the position going forward. After they traded Felix Mantilla, guys like Charlie Neal and Pumpsie Green filled the void until Smith in '64.

But the team was on another serious slide and looking like very little progress was being made. We still lost 109 games, the worst in the league for the third straight year. The 109 losses were two less than the year before, but that's not progress; that's ineptitude and failure. I tried believing things were going in the right direction, but it sure didn't feel like it because we had no identity. No real plan of action to make ourselves better. Guys were being traded, released, sold, you name it. To name just a few, we'd traded or released Mantilla, Hodges, Frank Thomas, Craig, Gene Woodling, and Piersall. It seemed like every time I looked up, somebody was cleaning out their locker and saying good-bye. We really needed some stability.

Chapter 6

ALL-STAR FOR A SEASON

WE ACQUIRED WARREN SPAHN in the off-season of '64, another legend of the game. It was nice having another superstar to talk shop with, but to me it was just another public relations thing the New York Mets had settled on since Day One. Another big-name star to attract fans to the game. And like Gil Hodges and Duke Snider, Spahn was past his prime playing days. He may have won 23 games in 1963, but his production dropped like a rock in '64, making him expendable.

He came over to perform the dual role of pitcher and pitching coach, reunited with Casey Stengel again after a disagreement they had way back in 1942. I'd seen enough examples of Stengel's temperament with a player, so it came as no surprise to me when I found out. But as our young pitchers flocked to Spahn for advice on how to pitch, I approached him for some hitting advice. That may sound like an odd thing to do, but he was a pretty good hitter, and he was left-handed. He batted well over .300 one year and he hit a decent number of home runs for a pitcher. We still had no batting coach, so what was the harm?

I don't remember any sound advice I got from Spahn about the art of hitting, but I was willing to listen to anybody who could help. As they wrote stories about him, it was brought to my attention. I was wearing the No. 21 he had for the Milwaukee Braves and said to myself, *I might as well give him it to him.* It didn't really have any special meaning for me. So I gave it to him in a gesture of good faith. When I gave him my uniform number, I expected the guy would give me a watch or something like that, but he didn't. Maybe I should have asked him first, but Spahn was kind of cheap. He didn't give you anything.

Turns out that was good luck for me giving him No. 21. In return, I got the No. 7 and I ended up making my only All-Star team that year. A lot of people think I took the No. 7 because of Mickey Mantle being my favorite player. But that wasn't it at all. When the clubhouse guys told me all they had left for infielders was jersey No. 7, I was surprised it was available.

Spahn didn't last too long with the club because he was over-riding Stengel at times. As pitching coach, he'd put himself in on close games to get a win or a save to improve his own record. He had so many career wins but was looking for more, especially anytime he could pick up a cheap win by coming in late with the score tied. That sort of thing. And when the young guys in the bullpen started complaining that they weren't put into a closing or a winning situation, Stengel and front office recognized the pitching coach part of the job he was doing was a mistake, so they made a change during the season. It's one thing when you're hired as just a player, but when you're a coach, you gotta utilize everybody correctly.

The revolving door of players kept turning before and during the '65 season but not on the scale I'd gotten used to seeing. The Mets took just one year to trade former All-Star outfielder George Altman to the Chicago Cubs for Billy Cowan, and by mid-season, Cowan was traded again by the ever-impatient Mets. That was another head-scratcher because Cowan had been a Pacific Coast League MVP. And he had all the tools, especially speed, power, and a strong arm. He hit 19 home runs the year before for the Cubs, but the thing with him was all the strikeouts. And Stengel didn't really give him a chance. I think part of that was the Mets had promoted a power-hitting outfielder named Ron Swoboda, and Stengel fell in love with him right away. After Swoboda hit some early-season home runs, they were actually comparing him to Mantle, so he became our everyday left fielder right away, leaving Cowan as a utility guy.

I didn't pay much attention to the guys the Mets had signed because of all the moves they'd constantly be making. But they'd also brought up Tug McGraw that same season. I could see how these guys could help us and was hoping the Mets would come to their senses and keep them around. By season's end, Swoboda would lead the club with 19 home runs, and McGraw would get into a lot of games, most of them in relief.

I wasn't looking too far ahead of myself and what the team could become. I had my own self to worry about and needed to focus on just that. But I started hearing some names of guys we'd signed like Bud Harrelson, Nolan Ryan, and Jerry Koosman, and with Cleon Jones needing more seasoning, I could see it coming together. As was the case in '64, I wanted and really needed to get off to a fast start. No more .139 for the first month or two, then going back to Buffalo. And looking at our Opening Day roster, the opportunity was there for the first time to be an everyday player at first base.

I started off hot and stayed hot for the first month and entered May, batting over .400 and at or near the top of the entire league. I had a two-homer game against the San Francisco Giants, drove in 13, and felt like it was finally coming together. Of course, I wasn't expecting to hit .400 all year but was still hitting over .340 into mid-June. That's when I hit an 0–31 slump that sent my average into a tailspin. I don't know what happened, but it happened. I was on top of the world when suddenly baseball—in its humbling way—found a way to knock me off my perch.

One of our early series was played at the brand-new Houston Astrodome. The "Eighth Wonder of the World," they called it. The first time I ever saw or played on Astroturf was in the Astrodome and I had mixed feelings about it. On defense you couldn't react fast enough to snag ground balls you'd be able to normally make on a grass field. My reflexes were still good, but on something hit hard, you had no chance. On the other hand, there were no bad hops and because of that fewer errors.

But they'd originally planted grass and figured the sun's rays would pass through the roof to give the grass sufficient sunlight, and it worked for a while. But the roof was covered in Lucite panels, and fielders at every position were losing balls against the dull color. If they took their eye off the ball and turned to run to the spot where they thought it was coming down, outfielders were sometimes missing balls by 10 feet. They took care of that problem by painting the panels black, which in turn caused the grass to die within a month.

After playing in the dome for a few games, I knew guys' averages were going to be 30 points higher than they should have been, and I didn't think that was a good thing for baseball or that it was fair. Anyone who played home games on Astroturf could see that. You could get a triple hitting a ground ball through the infield and watch it roll all the way to the wall. So you learned to hit ground balls.

But I wasn't one of those guys. Later on, I loved hitting in Pittsburgh and Philadelphia and Cincinnati, but I could never adjust to the Astrodome. It was the worst ballpark I ever played in. Yes, they had good pitchers, but even with the changes they made to the roof, the lighting was bad. The whole ballpark had a gloomy feel to it. Everything had a grayish tone to it, especially the background in center field. You couldn't see the ball coming off the pitcher's hand properly. I hated it there.

And before that they had the outdoor Colt Stadium, which had horrendous conditions when they were known as the Colt 45's. They used to spray the field in the fifth inning for mosquitos and they'd go throughout the whole stadium with these big guns, spraying God knows what chemicals to kill the mosquitos. It was awful breathing in that shit. Who knows what it did to you? But despite the dome and that awful slump, I got the average back up to .290 just before the All-Star break.

But the season and all the losses and losing streaks and being made fun of were beginning to take a toll on me. When you're losing all the time, how could it be fun for the players? We didn't enjoy all the negative write-ups. Guys that joined the team—who wanted to win like Ron Hunt—there wasn't enough of them, and after a while, all the negative stories would rub off on guys like him. Who screwed up, who made an error, that's what we read about. The writers would go to the pitcher and would ask why he threw such-and-such pitch that gave up a home run, nitpicking all the time. It was like that all the time. There wasn't much that was positive, but negative is what sold papers in New York. And now Stengel was being criticized, but what could he do about it? Stengel loved the young players. He tried to nurture us, but he couldn't get enough of us either to mold into a decent ballclub. We hadn't yet developed any roster continuity, and that was one of the reasons why we couldn't compete against anybody, let alone future Hall of Famers. You know why? Because we were Hall of Shamers.

We were mired in last place again at the All-Star break, on our way to 100 or more losses for the fourth straight year with no chance to compete for the title. I wasn't interested in any moral victories if we'd managed to finish in ninth place or have fewer than 100 losses to help boost our egos. At that pace, we'd never even be a .500 club, let alone contend for a championship. I was sick of the losing and sick of the culture of losing, sick of watching some of the guys accepting it. Don't get me wrong. We had plenty of guys like me who wanted to win, plenty of guys playing for a job. We just didn't have a good blend of young veterans. Instead, we had young and ready-to-retire veterans. And it never ended. There were no expectations for us. Everybody picked us for last place. All I knew was that I just wanted to win.

It wasn't as if I was moping around feeling sorry for myself, because I wasn't. I saw how the other clubs were building their teams, how balanced the league was from year to year. It wasn't like the American League where the New York Yankees were winning it every year. There'd been a new champion in the National League for six years straight, so I knew it could be done. And as hard as it was for me to admit, we needed to pay attention to ourselves by building through our minor leagues and not taking whatever veteran was available because of his name. As I was reviewing all this to myself, that's right around the same time when I got the news I'd made the All-Star team.

Of course, I was thrilled to be an All-Star and to finally live up to all the hype that surrounded me from the start. And when I saw the complete roster of names on the National League roster, I pinched myself. They had so many players that eventually become Hall of Famers. We had Hank Aaron, Roberto Clemente, Willie Mays, and that's just for starters.

The All-Star Games back then weren't nearly as organized or as commercial as it is today. We didn't have the Home Run Derby or any other fan-friendly events. You just played the game and you played the game to win. It was all about pride and representing your team and your league to show which league was better. It was important to the guys to win the game.

I don't think we had even a dinner before the game because guys were just trying to get to Minnesota where the game was to be played. You got there, went to the ballpark, worked out, and played the game. I just remember looking around the clubhouse and seeing all these great, great players and pinching myself again because I was one of them. There I was 20 years of age. You're not running up to any of them asking for autographs or any of that kind of thing. You respected the other players, and you gave them their space. If the opportunity came up to talk to a guy, that's what you did. The personalities of the players were different. You never saw the things that are going on today when I came up in '62.

I didn't get to bat or even play in that game and for that I held a grudge against our manager, Gene Mauch, my entire career. He hardly substituted at all, and on the few times he sent in a pinch-hitter, he never even looked my way. There were just a couple of guys who didn't play, and we all thought he hated us. Even his own player, Johnny Callison, sat next me the whole game. Even with Mauch being his manager with the Phillies and even with Callison hitting the winning home run in the All-Star Game the year before, he didn't get in. Imagine how he felt. It wasn't a personal thing for him not to play us; he just wanted to go with the star players. So why take me or Callison or any other player you're not gonna play to the All-Star Game? You couldn't even send us in for defense? How could you get into the game with that kind of managing? What the hell do I want to go to Minnesota for? I'd rather have the three days off then going there and just sitting on the bench as a rooter. You want to play in the game.

After that game I held resentment to Mauch my whole career and anytime I played his Montreal or Philadelphia teams, I wanted to beat him more than anybody. He was known as a great manager, but between what he did in Philadelphia in '64 and the way he managed the All-Star team, I couldn't agree. I don't think Mauch knew how I felt about it, but I never broadcast stuff like that. I just wanted to beat him. I tried to beat him, I tried to impress him, and at the end of my career when I was ready to retire, I got a call from Mauch in Minnesota to go play for the Twins. I retired instead of going to Minnesota because I hated Mauch for what he'd done. I held a grudge until the day I retired.

The early years were crazy, so many things negative happened against the Mets, and even something like not playing me in the All-Star Game added fuel to that fire. Aside from meeting the greats of the game and being their teammate for a day, the All-Star Game itself was a negative experience for me. But there would be other All-Star Games in my future. At least, I thought there would be.

About two weeks later, after another loss to the Philadelphia Phillies, Stengel lost his balance and fractured his hip at a local restaurant. He had surgery the next day, and when they informed him how long the rebab will be, he retired, and the Mets promoted Wes Westrum as manager. It certainly wasn't the way Stengel wanted to leave the game. But he was 75, and that was a serious injury.

But he was a good manager. He still had all his marbles and was alert. He knew the game of baseball more than anyone I'd been around. But he also realized he didn't have the players to compete and not much had changed in four years. But even with all the losing, he controlled the tempo and handled the press. He took the heat and loved the young guys like me and Swoboda and Jones. He had a good time with all of us trying to make us better players. We all loved playing for him because he was a player's manager who fought for you to get a few extra bucks. He really made things happen and took the pressure off the guys.

And I knew I'd miss some of the comedy that he always brought out in situations like the time earlier in the season when Swoboda struck out with a couple men on base and slammed his helmet against the dugout wall and almost hit Stengel. The helmet was on the floor facing upwards when Swoboda went to kick it again, stepped into it, and jammed his foot inside. So Swoboda tried to shake his foot out from the helmet, and Stengel yelled, "Get out in right field and stop breaking the equipment" while Swoboda still had the helmet attached to his foot. That was the kind of unrehearsed humor Stengel gave to the team. We needed some levity, and he always provided some. And we knew Westrum was more laid-back and conventional. He didn't say a lot, so the mood was far different now. We'd find out more about his managerial style later that year on a trip to the West Coast.

We were in Los Angeles on one of our trips to California and during the morning of the game, Swoboda, McGraw, and I decided to go to Disneyland for the day instead of hanging around the hotel room. Of course, we'd been in another losing streak after losing to Sandy Koufax the day before and we knew we'd be back in plenty of time for the night game.

We enjoyed ourselves at Disneyland and got back in plenty of time for pregame warmups and batting practice. After facing Koufax, it was Don Drysdale's turn, and he shut us out on a five-hitter, 1–0 win in which I had three of our five hits.

So now we'd lost 10 in a row, and Westrum figured it was time to have a clubhouse meeting. Well, he started ranting and raving about the guys being out past curfew and he started fining people to show us who was the boss. Near the end of his rant, he called out, "Swoboda, Kranepool, and McGraw, we found out you were at Disneyland all day. You're each fined $100."

Everybody in the clubhouse started laughing at that and thought it was a joke. A half dozen guys were being fined for being out past curfew, and three young kids were getting fined for going to Disneyland, so it became a joke because he was dead serious. But that's all we used to do when we were on the road. We'd go to the zoo in St. Louis and San Diego. We went to movies but always arrived at the ballpark early. Once guys on the other teams found out about it, they thought it was a farce and wondered why you can't go to Disneyland without being fined. It made no sense to any of us. I guess Westrum's theory was the sun was gonna tire us out, but we were in our early 20s. He was worried about us being in the sun and wearing us out, so he fined us. And $100 was a lot of money for us back then. That type of managing style was ridiculous and was one of the few times in my career I'd been fined.

They kept Westrum around for the '66 season and, as had been the norm for the Mets, they made an-off season transaction that included another big-time name. This time it was Ken Boyer. On paper, I didn't think the deal was a good one because we'd traded a much younger and solid player in Charley Smith, and a lefty starter in Al Jackson. And Smith had put together another good season for us and I thought added stability to an infield that changed every year. He'd led the club in RBIs and had some pop in his bat. But in the back of my mind, I knew it was too good to be true to not trade him. Jackson had a very misleading win/loss record, having been a 20-game loser twice in four years. But he had a good arm, and good left-handed pitchers were in high demand. But he wasn't the only guy with that embarrassing statistic. Every year of our existence, we had

20 game losers. And you had to feel sorry for those guys, especially Roger Craig, who lost 46 games over a two-year stretch. But when you've been shut out over 20 times in a season like we were in '65, it's surprising he didn't lose 30.

The Boyer trade was really unpopular in St. Louis. Boyer had been a perennial All-Star, a five-time Gold Glove winner, an MVP, and a World Series champion, so he had the resume, no question about it. And the Cardinals organization spun it off as best they could to a revolting fanbase outraged by the trade. It had only been a couple of years since Boyer was named MVP of the National League, but his production was way down in '65. And I looked at his age at 34 and knew that guys did slow down right around at that time and sometimes sooner. What were we gonna have him for? A couple of years? What everyone was hoping for was the return of Boyer to his former self. Maybe the trade would piss him off and he'd go out and have another MVP type season. Who knows?

Boyer had a good season, just not up to the standards he'd established. He edged me out for the team leadership in RBIs, but I had a breakout year with 16 home runs that led the club. But I didn't make the All-Star team. That distinction went to Ron Hunt, one of the few stabilizers we'd had on the club. Hunt and Jim Hickman were really the only guys on the club who you knew were going to play just about every day. But then the inevitable happened again. Both guys were traded for another star player, Tommy Davis.

Davis was a great hitter. When I first saw him in '62, he had over 80 RBIs, and this was at mid-season. He ended up with over 150 and wasn't even the league MVP, and now we had him. And as I thought about that crazy number, it was more than I'd driven in for two years. But with Maury Wills and Junior

Gilliam always on base in front of him and always stealing bases, you could understand, but we were still in awe of the number.

After I made the All-Star team, they started thinking that now I had finally arrived. But I was still only 20 years of age and I felt the pressure from that. My friends were still asking me at the time why I'm hitting .250, .260, because in the sand-lot I was hitting over .500. They asked me why I wasn't a star player hitting .300 and knocking in 100 runs like Davis. They'd known me as that dominating player who by now should have been an All-Star every year with much better numbers. I knew I'd let them down and I knew the fans and the organization had expected more of me, but I was still just 20, and there weren't a lot of .300 hitters around. But people didn't care to hear any of that stuff. The negative publicity surrounding me and the Mets never let up. No matter what you did as a player yourself, the press took the negative and ran with it. If I had a three-hit day and the team lost, they didn't write about Ed Kranepool getting three hits. They'd write about Joe Blow, who missed a ground ball or a fly ball, then tell you how the Mets lost. And the writers back in those days made fun of the team all the time. The one good thing about being around all these star players like Boyer and Davis was they offered an awful lot of advice on things like that, and they were very accommodating. So many veterans who came to the Mets had played on World Series teams, so you needed to pick their brains whenever the opportunity came up.

We were in a new stadium, and despite all the trades, the club was starting to develop new players. By that time, Swoboda was in the organization and Jones and Buddy Harrelson were up. Then Tom Seaver was acquired, and they had a nucleus of players, and we had a good farm system and a good scouting department. And being a bad ballclub, we got to draft early, but that distinction didn't turn out for us. Our draft picks did not pan out, and we had the No. 1 pick a few times. They picked Steve Chilcott over Reggie Jackson, and then Chilcott got hurt and never made the club. The Mets had finally paid attention to pitching prospects, and the idea was to develop Chilcott along with Ryan, Koosman, and Seaver.

Chapter 7

FROM GROWTH TO GIL

I GUESS THE BEST THING that happened in '66 was that we didn't lose 100 and finished in ninth place ahead of the Chicago Cubs. But that record could have been better. I remember sometime in August and into September, losing so many games in the last inning, close games that we seemed to always lose. (From August 11 to September 17 the New York Mets lost seven games on the opponents' last at-bat). To have so many of those kinds of loses in such a short period of time was disheartening. That takes so much out of a team. But we seemed to be more competitive than we had been before.

But that all changed back to our norm in '67 when we fell back into the cellar and lost 101 games. I'd had my best year to date and really felt like I was about to break out and even hit over .300. And Wes Westrum had promised me that I'd be the regular first baseman as long as my performance stayed the way it was or get better.

Boyer had been having some issues with his back, so they traded for Ed Charles to play third and later they traded Boyer to the Chicago White Sox. Charles joined the ballclub, and he was good to have around. He was a good player in Kansas City, but he was 34 and nearing the end of his career. After the Hunt/Hickman deal in which we received Tommy Davis, the

Mets picked up Jerry Buchek to play second and traded Eddie Bressoud after just one year as our shortstop.

All these guys moving around really affect the ballclub because you have no continuity. You've got to get to know each other because personalities play a big part of that. The good ballclubs had the same lineups every day, with guys batting in the same positions in the order. I changed batting positions all the time, be it third, fourth, sixth, seventh, leadoff; it was crazy. It was a who's on first routine, but it wasn't supposed to be funny. I took a look at all that, and since I'd become the regular first baseman, there wasn't a single year with the same guys in the infield. And the outfield was no better.

But I took another good look at the young players that came up through the organization and could visualize a stable lineup. Cleon Jones had a decent season, Ron Swoboda had a good year, and Bud Harrelson was plugged in at short and played tremendous defense for us. But the guy that was getting noticed the most was our young star pitcher, Tom Seaver.

Seaver was only 22 and had been in the minors for just one season, but you could see he had all the tools to be a solid starter. And he ended up leading the staff with 16 wins, passing Al Jackson's team record of 13, made the All-Star team, and was named Rookie of the Year. It was only the third time in club history one of our starters had a winning record. But nobody else on the staff had even 10 wins. We still needed pitching help and a more stable lineup. What we also needed was a manager who could change the culture of losing that had been around since Day One.

It was during the World Series when Joan Payson announced that Gil Hodges would be replacing Westrum as our manager. Since Hodges was still under contract with the Washington Senators as their manager, the Mets had to pay $100,000 to buy out his contracts and include a player in the deal. Apparently, the Senators asked for Seaver, but the Mets came to their senses and said no, settling on pitcher Bill Denehy. Turns out Denehy's only major league win came as a member of the Mets and was mostly a minor leaguer after that.

One of the first moves Hodges made was trading Davis for Tommie Agee. It was a bit surprising seeing that Davis led the club in just about every offensive category and was only 28 years of age. But Hodges wanted a leadoff guy with speed and power and Agee filled that need. And it was great for Jones since he and Agee had played together since grade school down in Alabama, and Jones could shift from center to left. And now we had our second Rookie of the Year on the club.

Like most of us, Agee had that sophomore slump, and the White Sox had lost faith in his hitting against right-handers. But he was beaned in the head in his first exhibition game against Bob Gibson, even being forewarned by Jones that Gibson would do that to a new guy, to show him who's the boss. It definitely affected his play after that. He hit an 0–34 slump, had no power to speak of, and for a guy with so many at-bats, 17 RBIs for the year wasn't what was advertised. Meanwhile, over in Chicago, Davis had an off year for himself, but his production was far better than Agee's. Looked like another flop of a deal.

But we were much more competitive than we'd been in previous seasons. We'd won more of the close games, but our bullpen couldn't do the job, especially in the extra-inning games, where we won only a few (two out of 15). Had we just split those games, we could have been a .500 team, but it felt good to not lose 100 or even 90. The biggest difference was we now had two aces. Koosman made the ballclub and just missed winning 20 and would have been Rookie of the Year if it wasn't for a guy named Johnny Bench. And there was no sophomore jinx for Seaver, who won 16 games again. There was no doubt about it. With those two guys on the mound, we had a good chance to win.

One of those extra-inning losses was at the Astrodome in April, another marathon game that went one inning longer than our 23-inning game against the San Francisco Giants in '64. I never liked playing there, and it wasn't only because of the bad lighting and bad background, but couple those issues with the good pitching they had, it was a challenge. And something strange always seemed to happen there.

We lost that game 1–0 on what was ruled an error by our shortstop, Al Weis. A routine grounder that would have ended the inning. It was a bad ballpark in every way—even the dirt was shit, so it was easy for a hole to form. Back in those days, they used to drag the field just one time a game in the fifth inning, so a lot of imperfections would build up on the field by the end of a game like that one. Since I was the Mets player representative, the guys came to me and complained about the conditions, so I went to Johnny Murphy, our general manager, and asked to have the rules changed with the suggestion that every five innings they had to drag the field. I said, "What's the purpose of going all these innings without dragging the field? It only takes a few minutes or two." So Murphy presented that suggestion to the league and to baseball, and the rule was changed.

Even with guys smoothing out an area near their positions, there were those other areas in the base paths you might not get to that would cause some problems. I'm sure many, many games had been affected by fields not being dragged enough. It was a good rule change.

That 1–0 loss was an awful game for a lot of guys. You'd go 0–4 or 0–5. You were mad at yourself, but guys were going 0–10, 1–9. I was one of the fortunate ones with two hits, but guys took a beating on their averages that game.

We had a brawl in Houston later in August when Doug Rader deliberately forearmed Kevin Collins with a pop-up slide at third, breaking his jaw and emptying both benches. Everybody was involved in the fray, and we got even with Rader when Don Cardwell decked him pretty good. We just seemed to have some bad blood with Houston. Maybe it was because we came into the league at the same time, and the Astros were always better than us, but they seemed to have our number. We'd only won one time at the dome in '67, and that's when I noted something strange with the air conditioning.

It looked to me like the A/C at the Astrodome was fixed, and to this day, I know it can be done. When you have machinery and you regulate the air flow, you can change it, and I think they changed it between innings by regulating the air flow to favor their players.

If you've got 20 air conditioners blowing in another direction that creates wind flow like it does at Wrigley Field when the wind is blowing out. None of us could hit the ball out of that stadium, yet Houston had a couple of guys that could do it. Granted, they had Jimmy Wynn and an aging Eddie Mathews, but they weren't the only guys hitting home runs or getting more distance with doubles and triples. Once I saw so many of our balls that looked like sure home runs going to the warning track, I started to get suspicious. I brought it up, but nothing came of it.

My year wasn't much better than Agee's. Three home runs and 20 RBIs were pathetic. As a team, we had a hard time scoring and averaged fewer than three runs per game, so the opportunities to drive guys in didn't come around too often. And I think because of that I let my temper get the best of me in a game against the Philadelphia Phillies.

It was late in the year, and Hodges wasn't playing me much at all. I was 0–3 against lefty Chris Short, and it was a bad 0–3, and he pinch hit for me. Being upset at myself and somewhat immature, I said, "If you're so smart, you should have done it four hours ago." Well, he didn't like that and told me to sit down in no uncertain terms. I was probably pissed at him along the way because I had a good season the year before, was having a terrible season now, and being platooned didn't sit well with me, so I just exploded. It was wrong to do that by calling him out in front of the club like that, so he reacted, showing everyone that he was the boss of the ballclub. I think Hodges was trying to figure out who on the ballclub could play, and I should have realized that, especially with the terrible year I was having. I wouldn't have played me either.

And then in that clubhouse, after everything quieted down, Swoboda went up to Hodges and started saying stuff like, "Gil, don't worry about it. My roommate didn't mean it." And Swoboda kept saying stuff like that to defend me, and Hodges went crazy on Swoboda, so he got himself in trouble along with me. Swoboda did a lot of talking like that, and that may have led to him to being traded to Montreal a few years later.

It was only a few days later when Hodges had his first heart attack and left specific instructions with Rube Walker not to play me. I thought about the timing of the whole thing but didn't think it was my fault. He smoked a lot. Maybe he wasn't feeling good and he overacted at me and Swoboda. Maybe he had something going on inside for a while and the stress of being a manager got to him. Who knows? So I sat on the bench after that and got just one at-bat the rest of the way. I could have kicked myself for mouthing off because then I went the whole winter wondering if I was gonna get traded or if they'd acquire another first baseman.

I had seen it with Casey Stengel and now I'd seen it with Hodges. But all the worrying over the winter never materialized, and we went to spring training ready to improve on our season, maybe even get to .500 for the first time.

But Hodges had higher aspirations for us in '69 and made no bones about it in spring training. He called us all together in an open session and said, "Watching you play last year as a team, you were better than you thought you were. We lost a lot of close one-run games, and that's the difference a championship club has. They win the close ones." Then he said, "You've got to think of ways to improve yourself so we can win more of those games. When you're close, you have to learn how to win. There is a way out. There is a way to win, and there is a way to lose, so if each one of you can do one thing to improve the club, we're gonna win more ballgames."

He was very convincing, and you knew he was right. But he was always that way. Hodges was a teacher and a student of the game. He knew how to play the game and he wanted you to perform at those levels. He didn't critique if you made an error. He'd ask why'd you made mental errors like miss a hit and run or the bunt sign. His philosophy was sound, and he'd played with other guys on the Dodgers with that same set of standards. And now he wanted to instill that in us. He wasn't worried about the Cubs or the Pittsburgh Pirates or all the other teams they'd pick to win the division. He wanted us to believe in ourselves as men and as ballplayers, and it was refreshing and inspiring to hear. A manager like Hodges was really a leader of men. He'd analyze each one of us and knew what made us go. And he wouldn't allow guys to make the same mental mistakes again. He didn't want to lose a ballgame if guys didn't know how many outs there were, things like that. Anything mentally that affected the ballgame, he wanted to eliminate that and combine that with the pitching, good defense, sound fundamentals that he'd built the team for. And that's why I say that he made a difference in ballgames. In the third inning, he was thinking about the sixth inning or what may happen in the eighth inning, having all the best players in the best positions.

We didn't get off to a great start, but a pair of wins at Wrigley against the Cubs brought us close to .500. More importantly, that sort of set the tone for the season rivalry after a little exchange of beanballs by Seaver and Cubs pitcher Bill Hands. Ron Santo had been a thorn in our side already, so Seaver played some chin music with him, and down went Santo, who was a bit animated and, of course, didn't appreciate the lesson from Seaver, especially after Seaver struck him out that same at-bat. When Seaver came to bat the next inning, Hands retaliated and drilled him with a fastball. Then Seaver hit Hands when he came up. There were no ejections or warnings after that. This was old-time baseball when things like this happened all the time. You expected your pitcher to even things up, show some guts, and defend the team. It had always been that way in the game. You did what you had to do, period.

It was no more than a few weeks later when we were in Cincinnati to play the Reds when I was involved in my own altercation. We'd just had a tough loss to the Atlanta Braves with a chance to win it in the ninth but left the bases loaded in a close loss, one of the few games we'd lose all season long like that. We won that game against the Reds with a big late rally. I had three hits and knocked in a run during, but probably the biggest hit I had was the left cross I gave to their first-base coach, Jimmy Bragan.

Like most altercations, this one started harmlessly when I took a throw from Ken Boswell to complete what I thought was an inning-ending double play. I flipped the ball to Bragan and headed for the dugout, but the umpire said that Boswell didn't touch the bag at second, so there were only two outs. I frantically asked Bragan for the ball, but instead of flipping it back to me, he threw it down the right-field line. So I didn't hesitate at all and clocked him pretty good. It all came down to the lack of respect we'd always been given, and this was another one of the times. When you heard and read about all the negative stuff that I'd been around for eight years, it didn't take much to snap like that. It's a lot of built-up emotion I carried around, so I was sending a message to the Reds not to mess with us.

Maybe those two incidents lit a fire in us because we did reach .500 after beating the Reds the next day and with a shut-out over Atlanta. We'd never been at .500 at such a late point of any season, but then it all seemed to be unravel with a five-game losing streak, including a sweep in Houston to the pesky Astros. Even with an identical record from the year before and Hodges stressing we needed to win the close games, we'd lost most of the one-run games.

We had an 11-game winning streak right after that, and I can tell you it felt like my sandlot and high school days again. The fact that we'd won six of them by one run was making Hodges look like a genius. Guys were contributing all over the place. First, it was Harrelson knocking in the only run of the game in the bottom of the ninth. Then Duffy Dyer got a clutch pinch-hit to win a game. Charles hit a three-run homer to win a game. Swoboda drew a bases-loaded walk in the ninth to beat the Giants. Jerry Grote and Weis knocked in the only two runs against the Los Angeles Dodgers. We'd reached .500 again and had come from behind to win the last four. The next night against the Dodgers, we were scoreless when I connected for a solo home run home run off of Alan Foster. An inning later,

I did it again, a two-run shot that gave us a 4–0 lead that held up. And just like that, we were over .500 (24–23).

The string of unsung heroes continued the next night when spot starter Jack DiLauro pitched two-hit, shutout ball for nine of the 15 innings the game went. Then a Wayne Garrett single in the 15th was misplayed by Willie Davis in the outfield, scoring Agee with the only run of the game. After opening that homestand with a loss to the San Diego Padres, we'd reeled off a string of seven nail-biting victories and our confidence was soaring.

But we knew as we headed for the coast to face the same teams in their ballparks they'd be out for blood. It was tough to win on the coast, and we'd be starting by playing the expansion Padres who'd put together their own six-game winning streak.

You couldn't take the two new expansion teams lightly like the league did to us for all these years. We'd only won five of the eight games we'd played against the Padres and Montreal Expos, and with the Padres being hot and being at home, something had to give. We were trailing 3–1 in the sixth when Harrelson and Agee started a rally with a pair of singles. Jones knocked in Harrelson with a force out, and I came up to face knuckleballer Joe Niekro. I really struggled with the knuckleball. I couldn't hit off of Joe or his brother, Phil, and it showed over my career. Surprisingly, I doubled up the gap in left-center that tied the game, 3–3.

We'd trailed so many times during our streak with so many guys coming through, and now it was Art Shamsky's turn. With Jones on second following another one of his many clutch hits that year, reliever Gary Ross intentionally walked me, and Shamsky singled to right to knock in Jones with the winning run. We added an insurance run in the ninth on a double by Agee, and our winning streak reached eight. Koosman stifled the Padres the next night with a complete-game win, and it was

Rod Gaspar's turn to shine adding three hits. We got the sweep the next day with another late rally that I started by knocking in Jones with a single in the seventh that cut the Padres' lead to 2–1. Then Agee doubled in Charles and Garrett singled in Harrelson in the eighth for the lead. Ron Taylor recorded the last six outs, and now we'd won 10 straight games.

To say we were ecstatic would be an understatement. We'd never been known as a team that rallied to win games late and now we'd done it a bunch of times during that amazing winning streak. And it continued again the next day in San Francisco, another come-from-behind win that turned into a rout, our first breather in a while. Agee hit two home runs, Cleon had a three-run blast, and even our pitcher, Don Cardwell, got three hits and the win.

You look at all those names making big contributions over those 11 wins and you had to start believing because it wasn't just one or two guys; it was the whole team. Koosman gave up just two runs over all the innings (28) he pitched. Seaver won a few times, Tug McGraw got a couple of saves and picked up a win. Jack DiLauro pitched that gem against the Dodgers. Gary Gentry won twice. But of all the guys pitching during that 11-game stretch, the biggest unsung hero was probably Taylor, who didn't give up a run in seven plus innings and recorded a bunch of saves (four) and wins (two) in his six appearances. Things settled down after that win. We lost three of four to the Giants and the Dodgers and, despite winning 12 of our last 15 games, we'd gained no ground on the red-hot Cubs.

But we were on unfamiliar ground. We'd surged ahead of Philadelphia, St. Louis, and Pittsburgh in the newly formed East Division, with only the Cubs ahead of us. We were in second place, still nine games out of first place, but Hodges' platform of each guy doing one thing better was working. We'd bought into it and new we'd seen the results. I was thrilled for the team and happy I'd made some key contributions during those 11 wins. I had 10 hits in the seven games and knocked in six important runs and, even though Hodges still wasn't playing me against the lefties, I was getting a good number of at-bats against a predominantly right-handed league. But then the rumor of the Mets acquiring first baseman Donn Clendenon from the Expos materialized, with the Mets sending Steve Renko and Kevin Collins to Montreal.

I didn't think the trade would affect me as much as it would some of our outfielders, namely Rod Gaspar. They'd move Jones back out to left field where he belonged, and with Agee a fixture in center and Swoboda and Shamsky platooning in right, somebody had to be the odd man out. But I wasn't sure yet if that guy would be me. It wasn't every day you got a slugger like Clendenon, and he'd been an everyday player for years with the Pirates. And being that we needed a strong right-handed hitter because we struggled against the lefties, Clendenon was the best option at the time.

What was surprising all along was that Hodges decided to platoon me at first base with Jones early on. Jones was a natural and gifted outfielder who wasn't a first baseman. Hodges really relied on his platoon system, but I thought he sacrificed a lot putting Swoboda in left when Jones moved to first. I guess I was lucky the majority of the starting pitchers were right-handed, so I ended up getting a lot of playing time and was performing well. Hodges gave me a few starts against lefties, but I didn't do myself any favors by going hitless against Woodie Fryman and Rich Nye. But that was a small sample size to judge anyone by.

After Clendenon came over, I hit a slump, (5-of-43) that dropped my average 50 some points. It was the one thing I told myself that couldn't happen, but yet it did. I might have been pressing when he came and mentally was thinking I needed to perform to stay in the lineup. I'm sure anytime you have a slump you start feeling it, like I did when I went 0–32 earlier in my career. And now we had this slugger who wants to play every day, and I'm making it easy on Hodges to make a decision. But Clendenon didn't help himself, either. He was probably pressing like I was, trying to show everyone why he'd been acquired. He didn't do well (4–of-25) in his first few games, and for the most part, Hodges' platoon system stayed in place.

There's been a lot of talk over the years about the Mets platoon system in '69. With the exception of Jones, Agee, Harrelson, and Grote, the other spots were usually rotated in our platoon system. Shamsky and Swoboda in right. Garrett and Charles at third. Boswell and Weis at second. Kranepool and Clendenon at first. But as the season wore on into early August and Clendenon got more comfortable, Hodges started using him more against right-handers.

In early August I started against righty Gary Nolan of the Cincinnati Reds and had a hit (1–4) then a few days later I didn't start against Milt Pappas and thought that was rather strange because I'd done well against him. I stayed in the lineup for a few more weeks, and then everything changed for me after going hitless against Gaylord Perry. I'd gotten my average up to around .250 but had only a couple of productive games, both against the Astros. And with Shamsky hitting around .350 like Jones was, Hodges moved Shamsky over to first to get some more offense. That move put me on the bench, even with the opposing teams sending righties Bill Singer, Jim Bunning, Clay Kirby, Rick Wise, Bill Hands, Fergie Jenkins, Bill Stoneman, and more righties than that. Even for the doubleheader when we beat the Pirates in a pair of 1–0 games in September, I sat on the bench watching another pair of righties, Dock Ellis and

Bob Moose. Only this time it wasn't Shamsky playing first base; it was Clendenon.

Why don't you play me against Bob Moose or Jim Bunning, or any of those other right-handers? I did well against those guys. I got only three at-bats during an entire month of pennant race baseball, the most important stretch of games the whole year. Coming in for defense in a few games didn't help me feel part of the magic that was going on. Nobody feels that by sitting on the bench. We'd gone from seven games back of the Cubs to the division lead and rattled off another 10-game winning streak during that time. Of course, I was thrilled at what was happening, but it was frustrating and a little depressing, not playing and feeling like part of the whole thing. You want to be part of something that was turning into something special, not sitting on the bench, hoping for a chance. I'd endured all the bad years and wasn't thrilled at my personal situation.

You have to remember that Hodges was still not in my corner at that point because of the fight I had with him in '68. I mouthed off once and knew I couldn't be that stupid to talk up now. And because of that, I think Hodges wanted to get rid of me and may have been trying to go behind closed doors. You could see the guys you did well against and inside you want to say something, but you can't. You don't play against all those righties. Who's he gonna play me against? I felt it was a personal thing with him and I didn't want to rile him up or get some bad press for the team during such a fun time. I confided with a few guys, but I didn't want to make a big deal over it, so I kept quiet and minded my own business.

But Clendenon proved to be the spark that we needed. We were mostly quiet guys, except for McGraw and Swoboda, so nobody really spoke up that much until Clendenon came aboard. He wasn't one of those guys who needed time to try to fit it because he was getting under the skin of everyone from Day One. But he did all that ribbing for the good of the ballclub. He just had that type of personality, and it was all part of his game. He gave it to you if you made an error or went 0–4, but it was all fun and games in trying to keep the locker room loose. And he could do it because he'd had some great years with Pittsburgh and had been around some great players like Roberto Clemente and Willie Stargell, so he learned from those guys. Jones and a few other guys would get on him if he was struggling, but he could take it as well as he dished it out. But he always came back with some comment that put things back on you, so he was quite proficient at deflecting things like that.

Clendenon came from an organization where the offense was the key component of the club and he noticed right away how things were done differently in pregame batting practice with the Mets. The Mets batting practice was hardly anything. We'd get 10 swings, and that was it. Clendenon told us the Pirates got about 10 minutes each and so he advocated for that. We'd all complained about it before, but nobody ever did anything about it or took it seriously. But Clendenon didn't let down on anything. He had a convincing way about him and the background with the Pirates to prove it. I'd always wondered why some of the other veteran guys we'd acquired never spoke up about it. Maybe they did, and I never knew, or maybe Pittsburgh was the only club that did things that way. Despite all the extra batting practice, Clendenon struck out a lot and became the scapegoat in Pittsburgh. He'd led the league a couple of times in strikeouts but still was a 90-RBI guy who could get you 20 home runs, and we were lucky to have him. And he was a good guy. He got along with every player. He was a players' player.

Chapter 8

QUALLS, CUBS, AND CATS

WE'D STAYED IN SECOND PLACE when July came around, but the Chicago Cubs had stayed hot and built their lead up to eight games. Then we got on another roll, winning the last two in St. Louis to split that four-games series, then sweeping three from the Pirates in Pittsburgh. At the same time, the Cubs had just dropped three of four to the St. Louis Cardinals, and we came home to face the Cubs, trailing by just five-and-a-half games but only three in the loss column.

Our offense was as hot as I'd seen it. We scored 42 runs in the five wins that started with a 14-inning win over the Cardinals, this time courtesy of Kenny Boswell's single to win the game and Wayne Garrett's four RBIs. But it was a game we thought we'd won after Jerry Koosman retired the first two batters in the eighth and then walked the next three guys that brought the tying run to the plate. That's when Gil Hodges decided to bring in Ron Taylor. I thought it was a good move because Taylor had gotten us out of jams like this before. But surprisingly, pinch-hitter Vic Davalillo hit a grand slam to tie the game.

A game like this one would have likely turned into a terrible loss for any of the old New York Mets teams but not anymore. There had been so many defining moments and turning points to our season, and in retrospect, this game was one of them. You can go through the games one by one and circle games like this one and probably be able to circle a dozen or more. As the season wore on, it just seemed that we'd find a way to win and expected to, that you'd look over at Hodges and expected him to make all the right moves. And when he made a change and something good seemed to always happen, you understood what a difference a good manager could make. Hodges had spread so much magic around; it was almost as if we were taking turns being the hero.

Our offense was on fire when we left Pittsburgh. We shelled the Cardinals 8–1 to get out of town with the split, courtesy of a leadoff home run by Tommic Agee and a complete game by Gary Gentry. When we got to Pittsburgh, the first two games were nothing like all of those 2–1, 3–2 games we'd played about every night. None of those scratching for a run like we'd been used to. Agee homered again in the opener, then we pummeled Dock Ellis and knocked him out in the second inning of the second game of a doubleheader before playing another defining moment game to sweep the series. By the second inning, the Pittsburgh Pirates had built a significant 6–1 lead off of Jim McAndrew and Nolan Ryan. But we crawled back again, a home run by Ed Charles cutting the lead to 6–4 going in to the sixth.

We hadn't been a team built on the big inning, but we'd just had a five-run first inning the game before, a four-run inning the game before that one, and another four-run inning in that 8–1 win over the Cardinals. It felt like no matter how behind we were; it wasn't far enough that we were still in the game and would find a way, somehow, to win. As was his usual all year long, Cleon Jones singled in a run with two outs to cut the Pirates lead to 6–5, and up to the plate strolled a very determined and very focused-looking Donn Clendenon.

You always want to show up your old team, and I'm sure that was going through Clendenon's mind when he came to the plate. I'd never been traded, but I knew how he must be feeling. I'd felt the same way since '65 when Gene Mauch didn't play me in the All-Star Game. I wanted to show him what a mistake that was every time I played him. And now here was Clendenon facing his old team in a key situation during a pennant race, getting showered with boos with the game on the line. I'd already pinch hit earlier on and I thought Hodges would send in Art Shamsky against the righty, Chuck Hartenstein, but he didn't. Shamsky had three hits the game before and had his average up to around .340, and despite the righty being a good matchup for him, he wasn't in the lineup. And that was the thing with Hodges. He went with the matchups most times, but he had these gut feelings at others. And when Clendenon connected for a long three-run home run, well, Hodges was right again in a magical season that defies explanation. Another one run, come-from-behind win and a showdown with the Cubs at Shea.

It was right at the mid-season point for games when we came home for a crucial three-game series against the Cubs. The New York Yankees had fallen from grace since '64, and when the Los Angeles Dodgers and San Francisco Giants were still in New York, New York always had something to root for in October. But the dry spell was in its fifth year, and now the fans in New York were going crazy for the Mets. But we still had our doubters. The press was asking how could we keep it up? That the law of averages would catch up to us, that we didn't have the powerhouse team like the Cubs to compete over 162 games, that our inexperience would do us in at the end, that we'd done it with smoke and mirrors, and our luck was about to run out.

And that's where Hodges was at his best. He paid no attention to the chatter and wanted the same from us. He was as focused as a manager can get and was never intimated by the likes of Ernie Banks, Billy Williams, Ron Santo, or Leo Durocher.

We all knew about the Cubs potent lineup; everybody in baseball did. But by this time we'd bought into Hodges' platoon system, and it was reaping rewards. Sure, we all wanted to start every game, every ballplayer wants that. But we wanted to win, and Hodges' philosophy was working.

There were over 55,000 delirious fans for Game 1 and we were facing their ace, Fergie Jenkins. Jenkins had been a 20-game winner the past two years and was on his way to that coveted number again. And he was in one of his grooves, giving up less than two runs per game in his last five starts.

It was a scoreless pitchers' duel between Jenkins and Koosman until I broke the tie with a solo home run in the fifth. I had never felt such noise from the fans as I rounded the bases and went into the dugout. But it didn't last long. The Cubs scored a run in each of the next three innings and went into the ninth with a 3–1 lead. Jenkins had only allowed the one hit and would have had a no-hitter going if I hadn't homered. He was mowing us down, so Durocher decided to keep him in to finish it. I could tell that the Cubs knew it was all but over, but by games' end, you could see the surprised look on their faces. In rapid succession, pinch-hit doubles by Boswell and Clendenon in between Agee's foul out brought the tying run to the plate, with Boswell having to stop at third on the second misplay in a row by center fielder Don Young. Boswell's double looked to be a routine fly ball, but Young had a hard time finding the ball in the sun and it fell in for a double. Then Young couldn't snag Clendenon's deep drive, and suddenly, there we were with the tying runs on base.

To say we were lucky right there would be accurate. The afternoon sun was tough on center fielders, and both guys had hit it right at a good outfielder. But Jones used to say he had a hard time picking the ball up when he played center. And now he was coming to the plate in another clutch situation he'd gotten so used to.

Jones was having an MVP type of year. He'd won a game in April with an RBI single against Bob Gibson, then did it again about a week later against Jim Bunning and the Pirates and followed that up with a walk-off home run in the ninth against the Cubs. It was still late April, but Jones was making a name for himself as one of the best clutch hitters in the league. Jones was the only guy I knew who watched films of himself after games and then started looking at other guys who were struggling and tried helping them. I should have taken a clue from all that because he was leading in batting. It seemed like every time he came up in a crucial spot he delivered either to tie the game or take the lead. So when he came to bat against Jenkins, I was as confident as a guy can be. With Hodges making all the right moves and Jones up again in a tough spot, I just knew deep down he'd get that tying run home, and he did. The third double of the inning brought in both runners and Shea Stadium to a new noise level. Then Durocher decided to set up the force out and walked Shamsky intentionally, and Garrett grounded out, putting Jones on third and Shamsky at second.

When I came to the plate in that situation, I thought for sure they'd walk me, too, which would have made perfect baseball sense to set up the force at any base. And being that I'd homered earlier off of Jenkins, you'd think they'd rather face the guy behind me, J. C. Martin. I even thought they might bring in another guy from the pen, but they didn't have any lefties out there. And in those few seconds, when everyone is playing mind games like this, I guess Durocher thought his best chances were to do nothing.

I didn't find it funny when Santo made fun of our infield and was ready to make him eat his words. It was sort of unwritten rule to not give your opponent any incentive, but with an All-Star-studded infield like they had, you could understand the comparisons, and they were many. How could an infield of me, Garrett, Bobby Pfeil, and Al Weis stack up against theirs? That's what Santo said. On paper, it was a no-brainer. They had us beat at every position. But you know what? The games are played between the lines, not on paper. Statistics don't tell the entire story. And maybe they hadn't paid enough attention to how we were winning so many ballgames in so many ways. Fergie had me down in the count 1–2 and threw an outside curveball that I lined to left-center, falling in that brought both Jones home and the house down. I was mobbed by my teammates as I rounded first base, and amidst all the celebration that followed, I snuck a peek over at Santo, shaking his head and walking off the field. It was the most important hit of my career as we celebrated the win.

We didn't call them that back then, but I'd only had a few walk-off hits in my career to that point, including a double off of Jack Baldschun of the Philadelphia Phillies in 1963 and a single off of the Milwaukee Braves' Bobby Tiefenauer in '65. You remember moments like these because they don't come often. Those games were memorable ones for me, but didn't compare to what this recent one felt like. And as it sank in that night, I couldn't wait to get back to the ballpark the next day wondering what was next, and what could possibly top that game.

I think all of New York was watching when Tom Seaver took the mound the next night. The whole city was alive and talking about us, and you could feel the electricity in the air when the fans poured through the turnstiles. Another win would bring us to within three-and-a half games, just one in the loss column, and everyone knew it. The fans knew it. The players knew it.

And the Cubs knew it. Seaver had been on a tear. He'd won his last seven decisions, including a complete game over the Cubs in May. They'd counter with lefty Ken Holtzman, so I knew I'd be on the bench in favor of Clendenon.

I'm sure Pfeil had read Santo's comments, so when he doubled home Agee in the first it felt like the baseball gods had responded. I looked at Santo, but he didn't show any outward signs, but I knew he must be fuming inside. Then, after Seaver helped his own cause with a run-scoring single the next inning, Weis scored our third run, becoming the third guy from Santo's list that had contributed.

You could tell from the outset that Seaver had some special stuff going for him. He was striking guys out and making guys hit weak grounders. And even when Jones stretched our lead with a home run in the seventh, all eyes were fixed on all the zeros on the scoreboard. That was not just a no-hit bid by Seaver; that was a perfect game.

I'd seen or played in my share of no-hitters by then, and it felt good to experience the suspense that builds from the other side for once. Of course, there was Koufax's on my fist day as a Met in '62, Jim Bunning's perfect game on Mother's Day in '64, and Jim Maloney's almost that wasn't in '65, a game in which Maloney had a no-hitter after 10 innings only to lose the game and the no-hitter on a Johnny Lewis home run in the 11th, one of the few times the old Mets spoiled anybody's party.

We left Seaver alone between innings, and you could feel the tension in the air. Hodges sent in a bunch of defensive replacements in the eighth, and Seaver retired Santo on a fly ball and Banks and Al Spangler on strikeouts. When Seaver came to bat in the eighth, he received a lengthy ovation, bunted Weis to second, and came off the field to a standing ovation.

Randy Hundley tried bunting his way on as the leadoff hitter in the ninth, but Seaver threw him out at first. We'd already seen an unwritten rule of baseball with Santo's comments and now this from Hundley. I understand trying to start a rally, but it didn't sit well with us. And had Hundley reached on a bunt, I think our bench would have emptied. I think he was lucky he wasn't called safe.

I think most baseball fans, and especially Mets fans, know the rest of the story. An unknown guy named Jimmy Qualls on a roster full of stars broke up the perfect game and no-hitter with a solid single between Jones and Agee. That Qualls ended his career with 31 hits tells the story of baseball in general. That you never know what you're gonna see or get from the game. That perfection can be ruined by an unknown guy with a clean hit to center, or a bunch of guys with names like Kranepool, Garrett, Weis, and Pfeil could help topple a Goliath. We felt sorry for Seaver that night. But he got it together and recorded the last two outs. More importantly, we'd won another game and we'd gotten the Cubs' attention.

We lost the next day after leading in the fifth, a Santo home run that gave them a decent 6–2 lead. Even being down by that many runs that late in the game, we'd proven ourselves time and time again and never felt we were out of it. The Montreal Expos were coming in for three games and then on to Chicago for a rematch with the Cubs, and we knew we couldn't let up. Maybe we were mentally exhausted from the Seaver game, but the Expos exploded and won easily 11–4. But back at Wrigley, the Phillies rallied for a few runs off of Ted Abernathy in the ninth, sending the Cubs to their sixth loss in seven games, which kept the lead over us at 4.5 games.

It may have been early, but you couldn't help but keep one eye on the scoreboard. There were still 70 some games to play, but we'd never been in this position before. That's when Hodges reminded us how long the season was, to stay focused on doing things right, to forget about the out-of-town scores, and that things would take care of themselves if we kept doing what we'd been doing.

By the time we got to Chicago, the Cubs had woken up with three straight wins against the Phillies and beat us 1–0 behind Bill Hands. And like clockwork and when we needed it most, Weis hit a three-run homer the next day in another one-run, 5–4 victory, and we knocked out Fergie after just over one inning in the rubber game, a total team effort of 14 hits spread up and down the lineup.

We followed that by taking two of four from the Expos, winning one game on a Pfeil pinch-hit bunt in the 10th, beat the Cincinnati Reds again on a two-run homer by Martin in the eighth, and Seaver took care of business with another one run win never the Reds. We trailed the Expos 5–0, but our four-run rally in the seventh made it close and we lost that one 5–4. We grabbed a 2–0 lead the next day to then Expos, but they rallied to win again 3–2. Then we committed three infield errors and lost at home to the Reds 3–2, and would lose to them again 6–3.

We'd floundered around .500 since that series with the Cubs at home, and they'd picked up a couple game on us in the standings. With the Houston Astros coming in for three games, we needed to right the ship and pay them back for what they did to us the last time we met. It was one of those baseball oddities that we had such a hard time with them. They'd swept us in the dome in May and came in on a hot streak of their own (eight wins in a row). I think the complexion of the season changed after they came in for three games, including a doubleheader to open it up. And after scoring 11 runs in the ninth inning of the first game, they came right back and scored 10 more runs in the third inning of the second game.

Nobody knew what was going on when Hodges went out there after a Johnny Edwards double down the left-field line that gave them an 8–0 lead. Edwards was the first guy Ryan faced after Gentry got pounded, so that was unlikely he'd make another change like that. Hodges passed right by Ryan and, as he got near Buddy Harrelson at short, I was trying to think what he could have done wrong. And he went past Harrelson and was walking rather methodically out to Jones in left field and met him near where Edwards' double had landed near the line.

I had never seen a manager do that before. It was wet as hell from all the rain that had fallen, and you wondered if Jones got hurt trying to run down that ball or if Hodges was scolding him for what may looked like a lack of hustle. So they stood out there for a few minutes, then turned around, and came back together to the dugout. Jones was hanging his head and walked a few feet behind Hodges, so his body language indicated lack of hustle was the reason he was pulled. So Ron Swoboda took his place in left field, and the Astros continued scoring. The 10-run inning was capped off by a home run by their pitcher, Larry Dierker.

You rarely see a team score double-digit runs in any one inning, and now they'd accomplished that feat twice in four innings time. With a pitching staff like we had, it was hard to watch them getting beaten up like that and even harder to believe they'd given up a week's worth of runs in just four innings.

The press was eager to run what they wanted to about the incident, and it was all over the papers that Hodges had pulled Jones for lack of hustle, and he was upset at how we'd reacted to the back-to-back shellings. But Jones had maintained that

Hodges took him out because his ankle was bothering him and wanted to stay in the game. Jones had been red hot, but here we were down 10–0, playing on a sloppy field with our best hitter nursing his ankle. It was probably the right move to make.

Whatever was said between Hodges and Jones changed our season around. A turning point for sure. Jones never said much about it and he kept what was wrong with him between himself and the trainers. But the players took it as a message that even our best player would be taken out of a game for lack of hustle. Hodges was saying we're not gonna stand for this, no matter who you are. Hodges' strategy seemed to work right away. We did lose 2–0 to the Astros the next day, then swept the Braves in fashion with consecutive one-run wins.

But Jones was out of the lineup with his bad ankle, relegated to pinch hitting for a few days. But he showed us in two of those wins how important it was for the team for him to stay healthy and to keep him in the lineup. Jones' two pinch-hitting appearances in that series produced three runs, including his single in the seventh that produced the only run of the game.

With all the guys contributing to so many dramatic wins, it was Jones who was the glue to the lineup. The season was exciting enough, but to see Jones' name at the top of the batting average leaders the whole season was pretty special. The Mets really never had a leader in any of the offensive categories, so it was good to look in the papers and see Jones battling it out with Pete Rose and Roberto Clemente for the batting title. If it weren't for that rib injury he suffered later on, I'm pretty sure he would have won it.

But in a month's time, everything Hodges had told us was coming true to the long season. The Cubs got hot (16–7), and we went cold. On top of that, the Cardinals passed us into second place in the standings. We were in a number of close games, but now we were losing half of them, and because of so many rainouts early in the year, we were playing doubleheaders once a week, with many others scheduled for August and September.

It was at the Astrodome where our woes continued with Houston. They swept us again, even after we'd led 5–1 in the middle game of the series. It wasn't as if the Astros were the old Astros because they weren't. In fact, they were much closer to the division lead than we were. They'd improved as much as we had and climbed to within just a few games of a very crowded West division while we fell back a full 10 games. They were dead in the water when the season started (4–20) and found a way to crawl out from such a giant hole and get themselves into the race.

And that was a good thing for baseball to see the two expansion teams that had been perennial losers for so many years finally start to compete. The Astros would stay close until mid-September but never above third place. Of course, we'd been glued to what was happening to the Cubs in our division, but you couldn't help but follow the West race that reminded everybody of the American League race in 1967 when five teams were bunched like this right to the end, or the National League race in '64 that the Phillies blew at the end. It really was a reminder that every single game counted. That's what Hodges was saying all along.

There were still about 50 games left to the season when we'd been drubbed by the Astros, and the Cubs, Cardinals, and Pirates were winners, and the distance between us and them was starting to show. Now we were 10 games out and in third place, closer to fourth-place Pittsburgh than to the first-place Cubs.

We opened another long homestead with the West Coast teams that started with back-to-back doubleheaders with the San Diego Padres, looking to duplicate what we'd done in May when we'd won the last seven games of that homestand on the way to that 11-game winning streak. You know as a player it was possible to duplicate that feat but not very likely. The Giants and Dodgers were in the race, and we knew we'd be facing Juan Marichal and Gaylord Perry and possibly Koufax later on.

But our focus was on the Padres, and they were a team in collapse. The bottom seemed to be falling out of their season just before they came in. They'd had a few long losing streaks and lost something like 14 out of their last 15. They reminded me of those early Mets teams with the long losing streaks, the blowouts, and even losing the close ones. But none of that mattered. Doubleheaders most often resulted in splits, and we had two of them coming up. We'd already had a couple turning points to our season, one that included that 11-game winning streak and the other Hodges' removal of Jones in the Houston game despite our losing record since that game. But within 48 hours, we'd taken all four games from the Padres, scoring just 10 runs in total.

Seaver went eight innings in Game 1 with a four-hit shutout. Then Grote knocked in the winning run with a go-ahead single late in the game to take Game 2. The next day Koosman went the distance, and Duffy Dyer hit a three-run homer to overcome a 2–0 deficit. Harrelson won it in the second game with a triple in the seventh. It felt almost identical to what we'd experienced during that 11-game winning streak, with a different guy as the hero every night. And we all got to play. Just as important were the 31 innings our starters gave us. Innings that protected our bullpen from being overworked.

Then we beat the Giants 1–0 on an Agee home run off of Marichal in the 14th. Shamsky hit a three-run homer and McAndrew throws another shutout, we lost a heartbreaker to the Giants the next day, then swept the Dodgers behind a

Swoboda home run, another clutch ninth-inning hit by Grote, and a bases-loaded double by Swoboda in the final game.

In the long up-and-down season of baseball, this was another one of those ups that kept repeating itself. It was incredible that we'd played such a similar homestead against the West Coast clubs than the first time when we started to believe in ourselves. Comeback wins and clutch hitting don't happen every game, but it sure felt like it was. And then we won six of 10 on the road trip to the coast that began with another sweep against the Padres before splitting four tough games with the Giants and losing two of three with the Dodgers. But the Cubs started to lose, and we'd cut the lead in half to five games. The Phillies were coming in for four and then had another showdown with Chicago.

It was right around this same time when I started losing playing time, and Hodges moved Shamsky over to first base for about a week. It was also the peak of the pennant race and when we made our move on the Cubs. And we weren't just picking up a game or two a week in the standings. It was more like a game every other day. At the same time the Cubs dropped 12 of 15, we'd won 12 of 14. They'd lost eight in a row, and in a week's time, we passed them in the standings. When they came into Shea for a two-game series, we'd cut the lead to 2.5 games. We took the opener on Agee's home run and Koosman's complete game. The anticipation of the matchup between Seaver and Jenkins the next night was on everyone's minds. Seaver had already won his 20th, and Jenkins was at 19.

We struck early on Boswell's two-run double, and Seaver retired the first 10 batters he faced. It was way too early in the game to be thinking Seaver could get his perfect game, but I'm sure that's what the fans and some of us were thinking. All that wishful thinking went by the boards on Glenn Beckert's double.

It was right then when one of the oddest things I'd seen in all my years of playing. As if by an omen, a black cat appeared and walked behind the on-deck circle where Santo was standing and then walked over in front of the Cubs dugout right in front of Durocher. And the roar of the crowd was so loud, the cat reacted and stayed there for a few seconds. Of course, people were taking it as an omen, and the press were champing at the bit to run that story. I'm not the type of person who believes in all that, but it was perfect timing.

No one knows if that cat was released by someone underneath or if it got spooked from all the noise from the fans. There were a lot of rats and garbage under the stadium from people throwing trash underneath. And the cats took care of the rodents that were there. I remember going down to take some swings, thinking I might be sent in to pinch hit and seeing all the garbage and stuff that would filter through and collect down below. You'd see a lot of dirt down there, and they didn't clean it very well, and there were a lot of cats—families of cats—hunting and scavenging. They moved around a lot, especially when the crowd made a lot of noise, and when the crowd started to roar, the next thing you knew, a cat came onto the field. There was so much noise coming from the left field area, I think the cat froze and didn't know what to do or where to go.

But it couldn't have been better timed. I mean, it didn't happen against Montreal or Philadelphia or any of those teams. This was the Cubs. This was Leo Durocher, the guy who had so much to say before the series started. It was a Hollywood moment for sure. Everything seemed to go in the Mets' favor, even something like this. That cat could have turned and walked in front of our dugout, but it didn't. It happened to be the kind of year we had. There were all kinds of crazy things that happened that year. We won on a balk. We won when the two pitchers knocked in the only runs in a doubleheader. Things broke just right for the Mets that year. Anything that you wanted to happen, happened.

What helped our season had nothing to do with us and had everything to do with the Cubs. On our last visit to Chicago, we noticed the Cubs seemed tired. By August their guys were very tired, and by September they had nothing left in the tank. Durocher had a tendency to not rest his guys very much, and with all the day games played in the Chicago heat, you could see some of them were getting bowlegged. By season's end they'd have six guys with 500 or more plate appearances, including a couple of guys with over 700. Even the bullpen had been overused by Durocher and was breaking down. Phil Regan pitched in almost half the games (71) with over 100 innings out of the pen. And Ted Abernathy (56) wasn't far behind.

It was a stark contrast to the way Hodges had run the ballclub. Jones and Agee were the only guys we had with over 500 plate appearances, and 11 of us played in 100 games or more. The bullpen was fairly balanced between Tug McGraw, Taylor, and Cal Koonce, so none of our guys were worn down in September. It wasn't really a surprise to us when the Cubs stayed losing like they did. We just didn't expect that total collapse that happened.

We moved into first place the next day with another doubleheader sweep of the Expos and the Cubs losing at Philadelphia. I'd gotten in as a pinch-hitter and for late defense in the second game, my first time batting in three weeks. And even though I was miffed at the way I was being used by Hodges, I bit my tongue.

I had 47 RBIs in the middle of August and didn't reach 50 for the season. I thought I'd easily get to 70 or 75, but look what happened. I was starting to think Hodges was gonna play out the season with me on the bench. Then when we opened up a four-game lead on the Cubs, Hodges started playing me against the right-handers.

Hodges was one or two steps ahead of everyone when it came to managing the ballclub. He had a knack of looking ahead of the game, anticipating what could or probably would happen. I think when he started playing me again, Hodges was anticipating the playoffs and that he was planning on going to go back to his platoon system with me and Clendenon. He never said it, and I didn't think about it at the time. But knowing his management style and trying to understand what he was thinking, I'm pretty sure that was it.

Five days later after Hodges started to use me again, we were facing Steve Carlton in St. Louis. The Cardinals had faded by then, so their hopes of catching us or the Cubs were slim. But I always kept in the back of my mind what happened to the '64 Phillies and what was happening to the Cubs now and that it could happen again. Carlton was as tough a lefty as there was and he proved it that night. And even with him breaking the all-time strikeout record for strikeouts in a game with 19, he lost on a pair of Swoboda home runs. It just kept happening. We won a game on a record night pitched against us.

Swoboda had worked on his hitting with our announcer, Ralph Kiner, before the game. Swoboda was striking out a lot as of late, and what better guy to work with in having Hall of Fame slugger Kiner give you some tips? Kiner would do that when he could, but for some reason, the Mets frowned upon him working with the players.

Swoboda had been a guy put into a similar circumstance that I was in when I first came up, and I felt for him. I'd been compared to Lou Gehrig and Hank Greenberg, and Casey Stengel didn't do Swoboda any favors by comparing him to Mickey

Mantle. It was apparent by now that neither of us were ever going to live up to that billing, but the stigma and the fading expectations would never go away. Since his rookie year when he clubbed 19 home runs and the soothsayers predicted more, his power numbers went down. And now, just four years later, he was a platoon player like I had become.

It was only a few days later when the Pirates' Bob Moose no-hit us. But we still didn't lose any ground to the reeling Cubs, and within another week, our lead became insurmountable, and the division was ours.

Chapter 9

ATLANTA/WORLD SERIES GAMES 1–3

WITH GIL HODGES' PLATOON SYSTEM, I still wasn't sure he'd play me against the Atlanta Braves' three righties in the playoffs. There was plenty of proof during the regular season that Hodges sat me on days a righty was pitching against us, so I didn't have a feeling one way or the other. I knew that I had hit well in Atlanta and did well against Pat Jarvis and Ron Reed and struggled against Phil Niekro, but with all of them right-handed, I felt as if I had a chance to play in those games.

Our best lineup was our left-handers against right-handers. Art Shamsky hit .300. Kenny Boswell was a good hitter and certainly better than Al Weis. Wayne Garrett was better than Ed Charles. So we had three or four guys who could hit who were on the bench lots of times when we were facing a left-hander. When we went into Atlanta, we knew we were gonna score some runs, but what we didn't see coming was our pitching staff was gonna give up so many runs. Atlanta had a great offensive team with Hank Aaron, Orlando Cepeda, Rico Carty, and a bunch of other good hitters, but nobody anticipated Tom Seaver struggling in Game 1, then Jerry Koosman had a bad inning in Game 2, and Gary Gentry barely got out of the second inning in Game 3.

I don't think we had a stretch of three games all year when our starters didn't give us at least eight innings, or a time when the offense came alive like we did. But that's all part of the equation that goes into winning. When the pitching is struggling, the offense picks them up, and vice versa. It was a good thing our left-handed lineup came alive and scored a lot of runs. If the right-handers were playing, we probably would have lost that series.

I was happy Hodges had me in the mix and had me starting all three games at first base. As usual, I struck out against Niekro my first at-bat, then singled off him later on. He was not my favorite guy to hit against. I didn't like trying to hit his knuckleball because the way he pitched me; he knew I couldn't hit it, and that's what he threw me all the time and rightly so. I needed a paddle to hit the damn thing. Even his catchers wearing those oversized gloves made for the knuckler had a hard time holding onto the ball. So why should he ever throw me a fastball? Had they had sabermetrics back then, they would have to have known all that and Donn Clendenon would have played instead.

We'd scored four times for Seaver, which was usually more than enough for him for two games. But the Braves broke through for five, culminating with Aaron's home run that broke a tie in the seventh. I think the Braves were a little shell-shocked in the eighth after Garrett doubled, Cleon Jones singled him in, and a series of stolen bases, fielder's choices, intentional walks, and errors plated a total of five runs for the Game 1 win.

We were up 8–0 in Game 2 with Koosman on the mound but hung onto the lead and won that one 11–6 on home runs by Jones, Boswell, and Tommie Agee. Agee and Boswell hit home runs again along with Garrett in Game 3 to complete the sweep. I didn't recall having any three straight games when we scored so many runs or back-to-back games hitting three home runs as a team. In fact, I couldn't recall any point in my career when such a thing happened. I don't know. Maybe it did.

We batted close to .330 (.327) as a team for that short series against Atlanta with Jones (.429) and Shamsky (.538) combining for 13 hits. I had my steady contributions with a hit in each game. And that's what I was good at during my career. I had a few long slumps and few hitting streaks, but for the most part, I was one of those 1-for-4 kinds of guys.

And now that I'd played in all three games, I was secretly rooting for the Minnesota Twins to beat the Baltimore Orioles in the American League playoffs. Not that the Orioles were considered by many to have the best team in baseball or the Twins were an easier team to beat. That had nothing to do with it.

It came down to the pitching. The Twins had righties Jim Perry, Dave Boswell, and Bob Miller with the only starting lefty being Jim Kaat. The only righty starters the Orioles had were Jim Palmer and Tom Phoebus, but in a World Series matchup, we knew they'd go with Palmer and lefty Dave McNally and Mike Cuellar. I wondered what Hodges would have done if the Twins had won. He hadn't played Clendenon at all against the Braves, and Clendenon was getting antsy sitting on the bench. But it wasn't only him. Charles and Ron Swoboda hadn't played at all either, and Weis and Rod Gaspar were used mostly for late game defense. Even Duffy Dyer didn't even get in as a pinch-hitter.

All the thinking was over when the Orioles swept the Twins in three straight hard-fought games. We'd be going to Baltimore to open the series against Cuellar, and a lot of those guys who hadn't played against Atlanta would be getting the start. Of course, I wanted to play, but I knew all too well what it felt like to be on the bench watching your team win without you. I was happy to see our righty hitters getting the chance, but we playfully reminded them how well we'd done against Atlanta and challenged them to keep it going.

There might have been a few concerns about our pitching after the Atlanta series, but there was a five-day break for them to get some rest. But when we went into Baltimore for the first two games of the series, we were listed by some as 100-1 underdogs. They'd gone position by position and gave the nod to Baltimore at just about every one. With guys like Frank and Brooks Robinson and Boog Powell, it was understandable. But we'd been under pressure most of the season and spent a good part of it trying to catch up to the Cubs. The Orioles had coasted from Day One. We felt that if we played those same types of games that brought so many late, exciting wins, we could take them. And we liked being the underdog. There's more pressure when you're the favorite.

Then Gaspar announced on Lindsey Nelson's radio show that we'd win four in a row. It was never wise to give the other team any added incentive, especially going into the World Series. But he'd said it, and we'd have to live with it.

That's when Frank Robinson caught wind of what Gaspar had said, and Robinson's comments reminded me of Ron Santo poking fun at our infielders earlier in the year when Robinson said, "Who in the hell is Ron Gaspar? Who is this punk guy?" He called him Ron! Didn't even know his name!

We never dwelled on what Gaspar said. But it took the Orioles just one batter to get on the board on a leadoff home run by Don Buford. They won that game 4–1, but we bounced back to win the second game behind Koosman and a ninth-inning single from Weis.

There's been so much written about the last three games of that series. But Game 2 was the exact kind of game we'd hoped for. Guys like Weis were referred to all year as an unlikely hero, but he wasn't to any of us. None of the guys were. It could have been J. C. Martin, Gaspar, or Dyer. Every one of those guys had their moments in '69. It didn't matter that Weis was a .220 type hitter, or that he hardly hit any home runs. Weis was a clutch player that had come through for us throughout the season. So when he singled in Charles for the winning run in the ninth, only the out-of-town reporters were surprised.

I got my only chance of the series against Palmer in Game 3, going my usual 1-for-4. I hit a home run off of Dave Leonhard in the eighth for the only World Series home run I'd have. It felt like I was floating around the bases, and the fans were as loud as I'd ever heard them before.

I was thrilled to have hit a World Series home run and I'd imagined it a million times as a kid. There's not much time to think about things like that when you're rounding the bases with 55,000 screaming fans cheering you on.

Playing in the World Series was what every player strived for. And for guys like me, who'd been on the other side for so many years, there was probably more meaning to it. I'd never even been close before playing for all those last-place teams, with most seasons 100 losses or more. I never thought it would happen, even after improving in 1968. I don't remember thinking about any of that when I rounded the bases, but I sure do now. It was on a similar level of getting my first base hit or hitting my first home run, but with what was on the line and with all the noise and cheering from the fans, it had exceeded all those feelings put together.

Like Buford did in Baltimore in Game 1, Agee blasted a long leadoff home run for us in the bottom of the first to give us the only run we'd need. The final score may have been 5-0, but it was the most misleading 5–0 game I'd ever played in. And even with my home run and Gentry and Nolan Ryan combining on the shutout, when it was all said and done, that game could have been called the Tommie Agee story.

The two catches Agee made that robbed the Orioles of at least four runs, maybe five, have gone down in history for Mets fans and beyond. I was in complete awe when I watched him run down those two balls and the way he covered so much ground to get there. I'm sure Ellie Hendricks and Paul Blair and everybody watching had those same thoughts.

We were ahead 3–0 in the fourth when Hendricks hit his drive to left center. My first thoughts were that Frank Robinson and Powell would be scoring and to hold Hendricks to a double. From his position in center, Agee had shaded Hendricks toward right, so there was no way he'd be able to track that ball down, and out in left, Jones looked to be a fair distance away.

But you can usually tell when an outfielder has a beat on a ball, and Agee had that body-language look. He ran toward the wall in left-center like a sprinter, and when he reached out his glove and the ball fell into the webbing and he raised it up for all of us to see, there was so much white showing that it looked like a snowball.

When Agee ran back into the dugout holding that ball in the webbing of his glove, you couldn't help but think later on about the great catch Willie Mays made in center in another World Series, the one where he's running toward center with his back to the infield and somehow made that catch. I'd seen that replay dozens of times and always thought that there'd never be another World Series catch like that one. But I was wrong.

We'd built our lead to 4–0 on another clutch hit from Jerry Grote, and Gentry was pitching a masterpiece. But after he got the first two guys in the seventh, he faced the bottom of the order but walked Mark Belanger, Dave May, and the leadoff man Buford. And just like that, the tying run came up with Blair at the plate and Frank Robinson and Powell after him.

Most of the talk about the Baltimore hitters was always about Frank Robinson, Powell, and Brooks Robinson, and rightfully so. But Blair had his breakout season that year and was capable of hitting one out, (26 regular-season home runs) or to keep the inning going for Robinson. So Hodges had seen enough with the walks from Gentry and brought in Ryan to face Blair.

I had always thought that Ryan had the best stuff on the staff. Everyone knew about his fastball, but his curveball was off the charts. But he had so many blister issues that affected his throws and at times had to come out of a few games because of it. Ryan hadn't pitched since he tossed seven innings of relief to get the win against the Braves in Game 3 of the playoffs, so he was well rested. But the layoff meant also that he could've been rusty. He could strike guys out with regularity, but he had a tendency to get wild now and then, and the last thing we needed was another walk to bring Robinson up with the bases loaded. But there would be no walk, or for that matter, no Robinson. What there would be was more of Agee.

From my vantage point at first base, I was thinking bases-clearing double when Blair connected on an 0–2 pitch from Ryan, this time way between Agee and Shamsky in right. But Agee was playing almost straightaway center, maybe a few feet shaded toward left. And this time, instead of bracing himself against the wall after making the catch, he went to the ground to make this one. Unbelievable.

They say that baseball is a game of inches, and what more proof could there be? Everything had to come together for both catches to have been made. If Hendricks had hit his ball just an inch more toward left, or if Agee had positioned himself just a few inches more toward right, or even if Agee's glove was an inch shorter, that ball would have landed, and our 3–0 lead would have been 3–2 with the tying run in scoring position. And the same goes for that play on Blair. Had Agee shaded Blair a few feet more toward left, that ball falls in. But in a season of miracles, the inches were with us.

We found out later that Agee's parents had flown in from Alabama and got there just before game time. It was the first time they'd ever seen their son play a professional game.

Chapter 10

THE UNSUNG HEROES

WE HELD AN IMPROBABLE 2–1 SERIES LEAD after two of the most exciting games of the season and most memorable in any recent World Series. Some of the writers and experts were calling us lucky, and that all we did was wake the sleeping giant inside the Baltimore Orioles, and that they'd come back and win in six.

We'd won 100 regular-season games, swept the Atlanta Braves in three games, held Baltimore's offense down, and had them on the ropes. Some reporters said that what Tommie Agee did in Game 3 wouldn't happen again, and that Baltimore was due for a few breaks, a few inches of their own. But what happened next in Game 4 and then Game 5 was nothing more than an extension of a season full of incredible, sometimes unbelievable games. I mean, with all that happened, these were games made out of some Hollywood script. Even now, when I think about it, it brings me chills just remembering how it all played out, of how our three outfielders made their mark, putting a stamp on a season of miracles.

There had been no guy working harder on his defense than Ron Swoboda. He'd have the coaches hit him sinking line drives at every angle, difficult ones for any outfielder to make a play on. He'd flop and dive around the field, trying to catch a ball before it hit the ground, but I don't recall if I ever saw him catch even one.

That's a part of the story and of that catch he made in the ninth inning that some people may not know, something that adds to the mystique of that '69 team. Here's a guy who had never made that play even once, and now in a crucial spot in a World Series game, he made it. For him to even have thought in that split second he had to go for it or play it safe, was incredibly brave. You look at that catch a hundred times and you still wonder how he caught it. And to then come up like he did and throw a strike, trying to get the runner tagging up from third, showed some pretty good concentration. I think that if that ball hit by Brooks Robinson gets by Swoboda, and even as slow as a runner as he was, Robinson gets an inside-the-park home run, and we probably lose the game.

The game went into the 10th, and Tom Seaver was still in there. He wasn't mowing guys down with strikeouts like he usually did, but he struck out Paul Blair to end an Orioles threat, setting up another improbable late win for us.

Another guy who'd done it all year for us was Jerry Grote. He started rallies, kept innings alive, and had a number of game-winning hits and he did it again with a leadoff double. They walked Al Weis intentionally, and that's when Gil Hodges made his moves.

Hodges was a champion at making the right moves at the right times. It was uncanny, really. We'd seen him push the right buttons all year and we knew he'd be making some moves now. Before the intentional walk to Weis, he'd already sent Rod Gaspar in to run for Grote and, with Seaver the next scheduled batter, he sent J.C. Martin up to pinch-hit for Seaver.

I suppose that Hodges could have sent me in at that moment, but because Grote had come out of the game, the natural guy to bat at that point would be the guy replacing him on defense. There was no point in using up two guys in one spot, and it is the reason why Hodges didn't send in me, or for that matter, Duffy Dyer for Martin when the Orioles brought in the lefty, Pete Richert to face him.

The way we'd played games like this all year was by moving runners over. This is when it came down to the chess match between managers, and even with Earl Weaver tossed earlier for arguing balls and strikes, the strategy would be the same. They issued an intentional walk, brought in a lefty to counter Hodges' move with Martin, and everyone knew it was a bunting situation.

Hodges had rubbed off on me in more ways than one, and I'd become very familiar with his mind-set and the mind-set of other managers in looking ahead to all the possible scenarios coming up. I knew he'd have Martin sacrificing bunting, and if he was successful and moved the runners to second and third, or if he made an out, they would have walked Agee to face Buddy Harrelson with the bases loaded.

And that wouldn't have been a bad thing either. Like Weis and Grote, Harrelson was another guy who kept rallies going. Harrelson was known mostly for his glove and was one of the best in the business, but he was also the guy who jump-started our 11-game winning streak early in the season with an 11th inning single for the only run of the game. You look back on games like that one and you remember things like that over the season. And as I saw the strategy of the game unfold in all these possibilities, Hodges left the dugout and met Martin on the field.

We'd seen Hodges whisper in a guy's ear before, but it took a little longer than most. In some ways, it reminded me of when Hodges calmly walked onto the field and met Cleon Jones way out in left field in that game against the Astros. I knew he'd probably told Martin to bunt and I knew it would only take a few words to make that request. But there really was something about Hodges and the way his messages came across. At such times when he's whispered into a guy's ear, it was a special moment between the two. There was nobody else who could hear what he was saying, no player, reporter, or fan. It was as private as it could get in front of 55,000 people. Hodges was almost like this baseball god that you wanted to please. And whatever his message was, I considered moments such as this one with Martin as a cherished one and was hoping he felt the same way.

The bunt Martin laid down was as perfect a bunt as you'll see. Richert bolted from the mound and nearly collided with Ellie Hendricks when he fielded the ball just over the dirt cutout on the first-base side of the field. I don't know if that near collision impacted his throw to first, but it hit Martin in the wrist and rolled slowly toward second base. Gaspar later said he couldn't hear a thing, but he rounded third and ran like a sprinter until he touched home plate. They looked at the replays after that bunt, and Martin was clearly on the inside of the lines when the ball hit him. But even after protesting, the call stood up. Another improbable win was in the books.

As rare and as unlikely it is for a game to end that way, especially in the World Series, what happened earlier in that game when Weaver was ejected for arguing balls and strikes was rare. Of course, he'd been known for getting in the face of an umpire and his theatrical tirades, but to see a manager thrown out in the middle of a pivotal game was surprising. I don't know if Weaver was trying to spark the team or what, but he probably should have exercised more control right then. I can only imagine what would have happened if he'd still been around for that final play.

Not lost in the whole thing was Gaspar scoring the winning run, the only run he'd ever score in a World Series game. Of course, none of us knew at the time how all those special moments we'd witnessed in the series would live on and become a big part of a guy's legacy. Martin would become known for his bunt. Gaspar would become known for his prediction of a sweep and for scoring that winning run. Agee and Swoboda for their catches. Who knew what awaited us in Game 5?

I couldn't sleep the night before that game. A million thoughts go through your mind at such times, so you toss and turn and you think about all that. I knew I wasn't going to play with Dave McNally on the mound. Donn Clendenon had already hit a couple of home runs in the series, including one off of McNally. Sluggers like Clendenon got into these hot streaks when they could carry a team for a few weeks, and he was on one now.

And we had Jerry Koosman on the mound. He'd already faced McNally in Game 2 and beat him 2–1, so we were expecting another pitcher's duel, another 2–1, 3–2 type game. Aside from the playoff game against Atlanta when Koosman had cruised through August and September and at one point had a bunch of complete games (five) in a row, we all knew when Koosman got the ball, the bullpen could usually take the day off. But in a series full of the unlikely, it happened again when Koosman surrendered a two-run homer to McNally.

There'd been some good hitting pitchers in baseball, but McNally certainly wasn't one of them. He didn't even bat a hundred for the season (.085) and was one of those guys you considered an easy out or a bunt and move-the-guy-over-guy. But we knew he had some power and had hit a few over the wall before. So when he connected off of Koosman and the ball landed behind Jones in the left-field bullpen, I think we all were a little surprised. As a side note and another comment on grand slams, McNally would hit one in the 1970 World Series, the first ever hit by a pitcher in the World Series. Go figure.

After Frank Robinson homered to give them a 3–0 lead, I wouldn't go as far as to say we had them where we wanted them. No team likes to have to come from behind, especially against a guy like McNally. You want to score first and build your lead, and the team that scores first wins most of the time. But there was a resiliency and belief we had that we would come back again, that we'd find a way to get to McNally, and Koosman would hold them down to three runs.

It's not every team you play on where that feeling prevails. That's how special that '69 team was. It didn't matter that McNally was coasting through our lineup or that he'd hit a home run. There was a belief up and down whatever lineup was out there and up and down that bench and bullpen that something big would happen. And like clockwork that something big happened when Jones led off the sixth. You couldn't tell that if McNally's pitch in the dirt hit Jones or not because Jones didn't react like it did. It looked like Jones was playing jump rope with the ball, trying not to get hit, but the ball didn't bounce straight back to the backstop, it came right into our dugout.

Most times when a guy gets hit by a pitch he drops his bat and heads down the line, but Jones didn't do that. He hesitated for a few seconds. Clendenon was on deck and the closest guy to the action, so he started jawing with umpire Lou DiMuro that the ball hit him on the foot. Yogi Berra was coaching first base and he came part way down the line to argue, and that's when Hodges came out of the dugout with that slow walk of his with the ball in his hand. DiMuro took a few looks at the ball and rotated it a few times in his hands, then he raised his arm and awarded first base to Jones. It took no time at all for Weaver to bolt from the dugout, and together with McNally, they said what they had to say.

I think that call got into McNally's head at that point. He may have been thinking about it and lost his concentration for a few seconds because a few pitches later Clendenon ripped one

I stand next to Nick Aromandi, who started the Castle Hill Little League I played in back in the 1950s, at the Polo Grounds in 1963.

Tracy Stallard, Duke Carmel, Steve Dillon, and I go to a New York Mets spring training dinner in 1963.

I pose for a picture in the late 1960s.

I got the opportunity to spend the 1966 and 1967 seasons with 11-time All-Star Ken Boyer.

I was solid in the field, but I really made my living with my bat and had more than 5,400 at-bats for the New York Mets.

I slide home safely against catcher Jerry May of the Pittsburgh Pirates.

Jerry Grote greets me at home after I hit my only World Series homer—a solo shot in Game 3 of the 1969 series off of Dave Leonhard.

I give Tug McGraw a champagne shower after we're crowned 1969 World Series champions.

I take a big swing against the Pittsburgh Pirates in the early 1970s.

In the early 1970s, (from left to right) Felix Millan, John Milner, myself, and Tug McGraw sign with New York Mets general manager Bob Scheffing.

I knew my way around the New York Mets' batting cage and dugout, having played in more than 1,800 games for the franchise.

I used this swing to hit 1,418 base hits, 118 home runs, and 614 RBIs during my 18 years with the New York Mets.

I stand next to former New York Mets general manager Frank Cashen while getting inducted into the Mets Hall of Fame in 1990.

Longtime New York Mets executive Bob Mandt (middle) joins me and Frank Cashen on that special day in 1990.

The Miracle Mets endure in popularity because of our improbable 1969 World Series victory, and I always enjoy interacting with fans at various team events and functions.

Though the New York Mets and I have gone through our ups and downs, Jeff Wilpon extended an olive branch to me in 2018, and that helped repair the relationship. Now I love being an ambassador for the team, but, of course, my true love is Monica, my wife of 40 years. (Photo on right courtesy of Ed Kranepool)

into the left-field seats, and we'd cut their lead to 3–2. Koosman retired the side and with Weis leading off in the seventh and Koosman on deck, I started playing manager again. Koosman's only mistake was the home run pitch he gave to McNally, but it was late in the game, and we were still behind. I figured if Weis reached first base or hit a double, Hodges would have Koosman bunt him over, but if Weis made an out, he'd probably send in a pinch-hitter. But there'd be no need for any of that. The Hollywood script played on when our "Mighty Mite" took McNally deep for a home run to tie the score.

I didn't know how many times Weis had homered in his career, but it seemed to me that they always counted for something. I knew he'd hit only two all year back in July at Wrigley, and both of those were key hits in those important games. Sometimes the stars of your team struggle on the big stage, and other guys like Weis perform like the stars, where they make a name for themselves. I think at that moment in time it happened for Weis. What may have been lost in the moment was Koosman staying in the game. Koosman was in the on-deck circle with Weis batting, and I don't know for sure what Hodges would have done had Weis made an out. Weis' home run may have altered the game in more ways than one.

McNally got through the inning, but his day was over. Koosman retired the side in order in the eighth, and when our guys came off the field, you could sense something good was gonna happen like it had all year, like it had in our three World Series wins. And with Jones leading off the inning, there was a good chance he'd reach base again. And he did.

Jones hit a clean double to start things off, then went to third on an infield grounder by Clendenon. With Swoboda coming up to face the righty Eddie Watt, I thought Baltimore would walk him intentionally to set upon the double play or bring me in as a pinch-hitter. Either way I thought they'd issue the free pass, but they chose to pitch to Swoboda instead. In hindsight, I'm sure Weaver wished he had.

Swoboda's sharp double to left brought in Jones for the go-ahead run, then Swoboda scored on an error. Shea Stadium was so loud that I couldn't hear myself think. And when Koosman took the mound for the ninth, the anticipation and the energy and the electricity in that ballpark was off the charts. The only problem being the heart of the Baltimore order was due up, and Koosman walked the first guy, Frank Robinson. But Powell grounded into a force, Brooks Robinson flew out to right, and Davey Johnson stepped to the plate.

Johnson wasn't the big home run threat he'd become later, but he had some pop in his bat. We'd already seen McNally and Weis hit home runs, so anything was possible. When he sent the ball flying out to left, it sounded like a sure home run. Even Johnson sort of paused, as if it was going over the wall. But Jones had a beat on the ball right from the start. He didn't even make it onto the warning track when he took a knee, and that final out of the World Series fell into his glove.

I've had over 50 years to think about all that happened in that regular season, the playoffs, and the World Series. And it wasn't just the fact that we won for ourselves and for the city of New York, it was for your average Joe working 9–5 because that's who we were. People could identify with us and loved rooting for the underdog. Our old fans could think back to when the San Francisco Giants and the Los Angeles Dodgers battled for National League supremacy in New York. We proved how working together can produce something special, that by playing your role, be it big or small, made for a brilliant production. Heck, guys on the other teams didn't even know some of our names.

All these years later people still talk about that season and that final game, of how outfielders named Agee and Swoboda made miraculous catches, and how a guy named Cleon Jones got hit by a pitch and then made the catch that defined that team for all time.

Chapter 11

THE AFTERMATH

EVERYWHERE WE WENT after winning the World Series, we were treated like royalty. You couldn't go to the store or out to dinner or a movie without being noticed. You'd take a photo with someone or sign a bunch of autographs, and people would cheer or honk their horns going by or give you little gifts. From where I'd been to where I was, none of that ever got old for me.

All that led to some of us spending three weeks at Caesar's Palace in Las Vegas, performing a few songs and saying a few jokes before guys like Buddy Hackett and Phil Foster came on. We weren't entertainers by a long shot, but every show we got a little more confident and got louder and louder with our singing. With the great backup singers we had, that helped us carry a tune; we started thinking we were better than we were. Our act concluded with the song, "The Impossible Dream," rewritten with lyrics about our impossible year. But going into the 1970 season, we wanted to prove to the world that we could do it twice, that an impossible dream can happen again and that now we were better than we thought.

After winning 100 games in '69 and winning the World Series, we all thought we could do it again, maybe even form a dynasty like the New York Yankees had. We had good pitching, good defense, and there was no reason to believe we couldn't do it again.

During the off-season, the press had run some numbers trying to put their fingers on exactly why we'd improved so dramatically from '68. This was way before the metrics they use today, but it was telling in so many ways because, as expected, there were marked improvements across the board. And as expected, our pitching was one of the biggest reasons for the improvement. In some ways, it wasn't a fair comparison because nobody was hitting because of the pitching mound changes. We'd scored a run more per game in '69 and still ranked ninth of the 12 teams in the league. We hit 28 more home runs in '69, yet ranked eighth.

It was amazing that we'd been in the bottom half of the league in almost every offensive department. But the stats don't tell the whole story. Tommie Agee became only the fourth New York Met to reach 20 home runs for a season, but with a platoon system in place, that came as no surprise to me. Ron Swoboda and Art Shamsky combined for 23, and so did Donn Clendenon and myself. And Swoboda and Shamsky combined for 99 RBIs; Clendenon and I had 86. It sure wasn't a perfect comparison, but for me, it told a good part of the story.

The other part of the story was getting a raise when your contract was up and how they went about the business side of things. Platooning may have been good for the team, but it wasn't for a player. You didn't go in there reminding them that you'd played half the games and had half the stats of a guy playing a full season. You didn't go in there with prepared materials comparing yourself to this guy and that guy. Hell, we didn't even have agents yet. What you did was listen to them tell you what you did have. They didn't care that you hit so many home runs or drove in so many runs. They told you the cold hard facts about your season, and getting any kind of raise was usually good enough. And now that we'd come off winning the World Series, getting a raise was on everybody's minds. Our share per player for winning the World Series was about $18,000. With my salary at $28,000, that was a huge amount of money for us. And when I signed a new contract for $32,000 before the '70 season, I felt like I'd hit the lottery. But getting back to the '69 season, it all went back to Gil Hodges stressing about winning more of the close games, and that's where the big difference was.

I'd never really paid attention to the number of one-run games a team plays in a season, but it averaged out to about a third of the games. It's a bit misleading at times because I never figured falling behind 6–0 then scoring five runs late qualified as a one-run game. In my mind, the back-and-forth games that stayed close for all nine innings or for extra innings, they were one-run games. The old Mets teams had plenty of those types of games, but for the '69 Mets, the majority were the back-and-forth kind.

We had a marked improvement of 14 games from '68 to '69, and our record in one run games (41–23) dwarfed the '68 season (26–37). That's when I really paid attention to winning teams and how they share that common denominator of winning the close games. Of all the statistics you can analyze, from home and road record to home runs and batting averages, it really all came down to the close games a team plays and how you did in those games. Going forward, I would remember that and look at that number at the end of every season.

And it went even further. We'd won 11 games in our last at-bat with nine guys participating in driving in that winning run. Important stats like these weren't on anybody's baseball card. They weren't used to get a better contract. They were just part of those intangible numbers, like sacrifice bunting or moving a runner from second to third with a grounder to the right side of the infield. And it was those types of baseball plays that we did our best at and why we won so many close games.

We did some wheeling and dealing in the off-season and released Ed Charles soon after the World Series, picking up Joe Foy from the Kansas City Royals to replace him. But it came at a steep price, sending Amos Otis and Bob Johnson to get him. I thought it was a bad trade from the start, and history would prove me right. Otis was a good outfielder and had a good bat, but our outfield was crowded, and every time they gave him a chance, he struggled at the plate. They tried Otis at third, but he wasn't an infielder. And with Foy being available, that was it for Otis.

But the trade made some sense at the time. Foy had a good season with the Royals, had a decent glove at third, and was still young (27). But this would be his third club in three years, and that always raised a flag with me, especially since he'd had a good season with the Boston Red Sox in '67, and they left him unprotected in the '68 expansion draft. Joe Foy was a New York player I grew up with on the sandlot and played against him in high school. The first guy I can remember to get in trouble with drugs. He got caught up with the New York scene, and it affected his career. Hodges had seen Foy play when Hodges was managing the Washington Senators, but somehow may not have known the whole story.

There was one incident late in the year when Foy went back to Washington for some drugs and he showed up late at the ballpark for a game. We all knew that was a big slap in the face to Hodges, and he'd probably bench him or try to trade him. Then he came out of the locker room during a team meeting, whistling a happy tune and drinking an ice cream soda. Hodges looked at him and didn't play him that day. And just about every Sunday when we had a home game, Foy couldn't play because he was partying and doing drugs on Saturday night somewhere. He'd be high as a kite coming into the clubhouse, so for a number of Sundays he couldn't play.

But maybe Hodges could see his problem was deeper than fining a guy or trading him. I think Hodges could see the future with Foy just as he'd seen a Game 3 innings later than the one we were in. Hodges was protecting him from the press and didn't want to talk to the press about it. With the press asking a bunch of questions about Foy not playing on Sunday home games, Hodges put him in at third for a game. But Foy was diving at balls he had no chance of catching and yelling like crazy at the batter to have the ball hit to him. Everyone knew he was mentally screwed up because of the drugs. Hodges took him out of the ballgame but not right away. We all could tell that Foy didn't fit in with the team, and the press figured it out and they wrote a story about it. After the 1970 season, Foy went drafted by the Senators in the Rule 5 draft, got released in May, and was out of baseball for good. From a purely baseball standpoint, it was really too bad that the drugs were the cause of such a short career. Foy could have been the fixture at third we'd always been after.

But I hadn't been around to see much of that '70 season, and that surprised me. I wasn't worried at all about making the team in spring training or getting traded like I had the year before after I argued with Hodges in Philadelphia at the end of '68. I think they had one deal when we were in Lakeland in '69 that I was gonna be traded to the Detroit Tigers that day and was literally looking over my shoulder every inning, waiting for somebody to tap me on the shoulder and say you're traded. I knew if that happened, I wasn't taking Norm Cash's job at first anytime soon. He was around 35 years of age and still putting up decent numbers. As it turned out, I think the front office decided not to trade me yet, even though Hodges wanted to get rid of me.

I started only five games before Hodges used me mostly as a pinch-hitter after that and I didn't adjust well to the role. I think I was 0–18 as a pinch-hitter and with the lack of playing time I was barely hitting .100. And with Clendenon playing every day and batting .300, the writing was on the wall.

So they said you better go down to the minors and get your batting average back. I knew they had some young players coming up like Ken Singleton, so I figured it was a good time to showcase my talents and maybe attract some other teams. But deep down I wanted to stay a Met despite all the obstacles that kept coming my way. I was still just 25 and in my eighth year with the club, so I had my prime years ahead of me. I knew I had to stay positive and not let such a giant blow to my ego get in the way of results. I knew I had to show the ballclub that you're better than what they think you are and that I had to produce. That's what I had to do. Before I went down, Donald Grant told me to go down there and show him what I could do. So I asked him If I went down and did well, would you bring me back to the major leagues? And he said he would.

At that point, I actually considered retiring, but I was too young to retire. I knew Hodges didn't want me on the ballclub and I felt I was screwed and unwelcome at the same time. I thought about it some more, and a part of me really wanted to quit. But the more I spoke with Grant and he promised me I'd come back if I did well, the more I wanted to stay and to try. I liked Grant because he was a man of his word—a businessman. If he shook your hand, you could go to the bank with it. So I said to him exactly what was going on, that I wasn't getting along with Hodges and what happened between us in Philadelphia. I said Hodges was never gonna call me back to the major leagues, but Grant said, "Look, do yourself a favor. Shut your mouth. Go to the minor leagues and show them with your bat that you belong in the major leagues, and I will guarantee you I will get you back to the major leagues." I shook his hand and I went to the minor leagues that same day.

I knew I would have been a better player had they kept me in the minors for a few years right from the start. I would have been a better player because I wouldn't have exposed myself to the fans of New York right away, and now after six years, they thought I was over the hill and hadn't become a star player. That had always been hard for me to overcome, and I was reminded about it constantly. And then I was back in the minors, fighting for a foothold. The most credit I can give to myself was when I went down and fought back under terrible circumstances. A manager who didn't like you and wanted to trade you was a bad spot to be in, and the fans getting on me because I hadn't developed was hard on me.

The one goal I had was to play every day in the minor leagues and to hit well, and I did. My only thought was getting back to the major leagues. I wasn't concerned about the Mets at that point and where they might be in the standings. I was hoping to showcase myself and do well and then come back to New York or get traded to another team. So I did go to Tidewater and did quite well. I drove in 45 runs in 47 games, batted over .300, and played every day at first base. And with the Mets locked in another pennant race, they brought me back up in August.

I had been so focused on myself and the team in Tidewater, I barely followed the standings in baseball. But I knew the Mets were close to the Pittsburgh Pirates, and the Chicago Cubs were right behind. I wasn't sure how Hodges was planning to use me, and it didn't matter to me if I was at first or in the outfield. I just wanted to play. But they had a nice rotation going with Clendenon, Shamsky, Swoboda, the rookie Singleton, and even Mike Jorgensen. With Cleon Jones and Agee holding down two of the outfield spots, and all the other guys doing well, and in the mix, I was probably going to be the odd man out and I was right. I stayed on the bench for the rest of the year. It felt no different to me when Hodges benched me during the year before when we made our move on the Cubs. You're on the team, but when you're not playing much, you feel isolated because in some ways you are. You're cheering on your teammates, but it's not the same feeling compared to being on the field.

I think our fans were ready to see a little of the magic from '69 and probably expected it. We hadn't won anything close to the 100 wins and hadn't had as many of the late rallies and drama. Those last two weeks proved to be nothing like '69. We lost three of four games at home to the Pirates, then got swept by them a few days later in Pittsburgh. And with five of those six losses by one run, the magic from '69 was gone. No great comebacks to save the season. And all I did was pinch-hit and play some late defense after I returned. Not one start at all and an embarrassing total of plate appearances as a pinch-hitter (33) or late-game substitute.

And I didn't like pinch-hitting and couldn't adjust to getting one at-bat here and there. If it wasn't for a stretch of three late games when I had a pinch-hit in each appearance, my final average (.170) would have been around .100. I wasn't happy at all sitting on the bench. I went down to the minors and had a good season, so I knew I could have contributed. And there's so many factors that make a season. Maybe we were making more mental mistakes than we did in '69. The relief pitching and the starters weren't as strong. Clutch hitting

and some luck weren't with us as often. Injuries to a bunch
of guys. Plus, everyone was gunning for us as the champions.
They wanted to beat us.

The 1970 year was the toughest for me because I didn't see
it coming. You're a major leaguer for a long time, then you've
won a World Series, and just like that, you're in the minors.
That's tough to adjust to, very tough. You can give up if you're
a quitter, but I didn't quit. I developed in the minor leagues,
and it helped me become a better hitter, but I was still catching
up with the league. I was the age most guys usually made it to
the major leagues, and I had seven-plus years in the league by
then. You hate to blame them for how they handled me from
the start, but they ruined my career by bringing me up early,
exposing me, sending me back down, and breaking my spirit.
Then you gotta come back and play. In hindsight, I should have
been a better player and know I would have been if they'd let
me develop in the minor leagues for two to three years with
other young guys around my age. I believe I would have excelled
in the major leagues.

But Hodges gave me no chance to play, and Clendenon had
a good year. I was convinced more than ever that I'd be traded
in the off-season. What else could they do with me? Send me
back to the minors? Put me on the bench? I'm sure my trade
value had dropped, but in my mind, it was gonna happen. They'd
already traded Otis, Johnson, Rod Gaspar, J.C Martin, Bobby
Pfeil, and sold Cal Koonce and Don Cardwell, all members of
that '69 club. And they brought in Bob Aspromonte to take
Foy's place at third, another stopgap third baseman at the end
of his career. I'd seen the way the club moved guys around, so
I was expecting I'd be next. But it wasn't me who was next. It
was Swoboda.

Everyone knew they'd be grooming the switch-hitting Singleton for right field, especially after what he showed them in '70. And Swoboda had a tendency to run his mouth, even after the day he defended me in Philadelphia. I'd learned from that to not lash out at difficult times, but Swoboda spoke up all the time. He complained about the Mets contract offer to him after the World Series, then campaigned for himself to get more playing time or be traded. With how Hodges reacted to such things, I didn't think it was wise of Swoboda to take a stand like that. Giving Hodges an ultimatum was professional suicide. And Swoboda found out the hard way, getting dealt to the Montreal Expos on the last day of spring training.

Swoboda may have gotten his wish to be traded, but he was playing less with the Expos than with the Mets. He hardly played at all with Montreal, and I knew he was disgruntled being there and probably wished he never said a word about his playing time in New York. It wasn't three months later when the Expos peddled him back to New York—this time as a Yankee. But the New York Yankees had an even more solid outfield than the Expos had, and in less than three years, including the advent of the designated hitter in '73, Swoboda couldn't crack that lineup, never getting back to the player he was with the Mets.

Swoboda and I were roommates before the trade, so we had a lot of things to talk about. And I was glad he was back in New York because we'd become partners in a restaurant we had built on Long Island, near where both of us lived, right after the '69 series.

And after the World Series win, we thought it was a good idea after speaking to my next-door neighbor about it. He was an architect and businessman and he designed the building from the ground up. It was a beautiful steak and lobster house with a circular bar, great tables, and a sports theme with the ballgames on during the nighttime and during the school year. It was a great place for kids to come with their families for birthdays and autograph signings from some of the players. The Mets were excited for us, and we held different promos we thought were inventive and good for business. If one of us got a home run, we'd buy a round for the house. It was five minutes from my house and 20 from Swoboda's, and we took turns visiting it, saying hello to customers, that kind of thing.

We learned soon enough it was tough to control things, especially with us absent so often. We hired a manager and we had capable people and friends working there, so we thought that was enough to run a business. After a while, we found out how green we were about running a business, especially the restaurant business. We made some poor decisions and worked our way through it, learning as we grew. It was a tough business. With all our inventory and liquor, you had to watch everything, but we couldn't. We had employees asking for raises minutes before opening the doors on a booked Friday night. They'd argue with you before dinner, putting you on the spot. We learned that running a restaurant required a lot of hours by someone who knew the industry, and with us being gone so often, that became a problem. And because of our lack of experience, we created some of the problems ourselves and learned the hard way it's not just serving a good meal, saying hello, and making people happy that constitute running a business.

As time went on, we weren't making as much money as we thought we would and started having other problems. Unions were coming in and dictating who we had to hire, and we couldn't fire people if we thought they needed to be fired. The labor board told me in one of the meetings we hadn't followed the proper protocols, and I was surprised because we owned the place. That's when I knew I had a lot to learn for sure. With all the labor problems and assorted other problems, it wasn't worth the aggravation anymore, so we decided to sell the building and the property.

When Swoboda got traded to Montreal, it all fell on me, so I was happy the Expos traded him to the Yankees. But even when we were together, we didn't confide in each other like we should have, and Swoboda didn't know at times what was going on. There was one time when Swoboda went down to the freezer around four in the afternoon to check the meat, and the next thing you know, I get a phone call from him, and he's very upset that the very expensive meat we'd purchased was hanging in the freezer looking rancid. And sometimes he reacted first and asked question later, so instead of confronting the chef, he trashed all the meat, wanting to make an example out of the chef. But what Swoboda didn't realize was the chef was aging the meat to become our prime steaks.

We had 150-200 reservations that night and pissed off the chef, who reacted by saying he was going home. It taught us a lesson not to get involved in something you know nothing about. It was inexperience at its best. We knew we had to make some changes, and we did. We fired ourselves!

I wasn't directly involved with that fight with the chef, but I was with teammate Tim Foli in May. What started off with me throwing some routine grounders to the infielders between innings escalated into a fight between us in the dugout when the inning was over. Foli was a high-strung player, a very aggressive player, and did everything right in the field. He had a short fuse and let hold emotions get the best of him sometimes. We gave him the name, "Crazy Horse" because of all that.

I was throwing the ball around to second, to short, to third, and every time Foli got the ball—he would fling it over my head and into the stands and even hit somebody in the stands. He was just so temperamental and high strung. Maybe he was mad from the previous at-bat and thinking about that instead of playing defense because none of his throws were even close. Next thing you know, his next throw went in the dirt, bounced up and hits, me in the chest, and then he did it again. I finally said to him, "Hey I'm not gonna throw you the ball if you're gonna throw your shit into the stands and into the dirt. I'm not gonna be used for target practice for you. Take it out on the pitcher, don't take it out on me. I'm not getting you out. I'm on your side. I've got my own problems."

So we came in at the end of the inning and we got into the dugout and he came up toward me and started yelling, "You gotta throw me the ball, that's not right!" And I said, "I don't have to throw you the ball because you don't throw it across the diamond like a normal infielder, and I'm not gonna allow you to do that."

So he came closer and closer and I said, "Tim, you better stay away from me," and he kept saying "You gotta throw me the ball," and then he tapped me on my chest with his two fingers like he's trying to make his point. So I said, "You better stay away because if you do it again you're gonna have a problem." So he went to tap me again on the chest, and I took a swing and knocked him out with one punch to the head. I was from New York, and you don't have people threaten you and ask questions later. You can't take any shit from anyone because everybody struggles. He's picking on a guy that struggled five-to-six years himself, so you don't need somebody poking on your chest and trying to show you up in front of your teammates. Didn't make any sense.

He was slumped over on the steps of the dugout, and I was gonna clock him again, but the guys grabbed me before I could.

I'm glad they did because the way his head was wedged between the steps another punch could have fractured his head or even killed him. That was fortunate for both of us. Our teammates stepped in to stop the whole thing. Almost immediately, he got this big black, swollen eye, and that's when Hodges came running over.

I was thinking the worst for myself, that there was a chance that this is where things change again, and none of it was any good. It seemed to me it was the perfect time for Hodges do something drastic, maybe fine me or take me out of the ballgame, or send me back to the minors or step up any trade talks they may have been having with other clubs. So Hodges looked down at Foli, still lying on the floor with his swollen, black eye, and Hodges said in no uncertain terms, "Timmy, you better go on the field at the end of the inning. And if you can't get on the field, you're gonna be in trouble." So now I'm surprised and relieved at what Hodges said, but he's not finished. Hodges turns back to Foli and yells out, "If I was Ed, I wouldn't throw you the ball either!"

That made me look good in front of all the players because he took my side, and it was the first time in a couple years he'd stuck up for me. Hodges wasn't the kind of manager who'd actually say things are good now. But I knew that as long as I performed and didn't mouth off, from that point on, he was in my corner. Once he supported me like that, I knew we were on better terms again.

That showed me that Hodges could forget. If you produced for him on the field, he was not a guy that was gonna hold a grudge forever. In his own mind, he knew what I'd been through the last couple of years, that I worked my ass off to get back to New York, and proved I can play. Instead of showing him how soft he may have thought I was, I showed him I could take the hard road and get my act together. He didn't say any of this with the Foli incident, but that's what I read into it. He was the boss, and even though it took me some time to realize it, he made me a better player.

Chapter 12

TRADES, FADES, AND
AVERAGE GRADES

WE HAD SOMETHING TO PROVE IN 1971, but trying to duplicate what we did in 1969 was easier said than done, and that was proven in 1970. Through mid-June we'd bounced back and forth between first and second place, then had a rough two weeks that put us way behind the Pittsburgh Pirates. But we weren't playing anywhere near the close games we'd played in 1969. We only had a couple of close games in all those losses and didn't win one. We'd fallen behind in most of those games and, in the few games we had the lead, we couldn't hold it. By then, we'd lost a lot of ground in the standings to the red-hot Pirates, and it kept getting worse.

You couldn't put your finger on any one thing that year, but it no longer felt like what we had experienced in '69 when we thought we were building a dynasty. We'd thought we'd be in the World Series again in '70 and have a competitive club year in and year out for some time. But now it was the Pirates who'd won the East two years in a row, not us. It was a down year for the club, but I bounced back and had my best year as a pro. I had a shot at .300 but finished the season with a 1-for-15 final push and ended at .280 with the most RBIs I'd had (58) in any one season.

One of the reasons I lifted my average besides getting more playing time was the new parks that had come into the league. Being a line-drive, ground ball type hitter, the new turf stadiums in cities like Philadelphia, Cincinnati, and Pittsburgh were all about the hitter and were where I did some of my best hitting. As an infielder, I didn't like the tartan turf they had in Pittsburgh. It was more like a rug and when it got wet, the ball would skid through. Three Rivers was great for hitters.

Connie Mack in Philadelphia was a more normal stadium, but it had really low dugouts. If you stood up fast, you'd wind up hitting your head on that low dugout, so everyone had to be careful. Right-handers liked playing there. Forbes Field in Pittsburgh was a terrible field with a hard infield with a lot of rocks. Look what happened to Tony Kubek in the 1960 World series with a bad hop that hit him in the throat. I refused to take infield practice there because there were so many rocks and pebbles. That was like a graveyard out there. I hated playing on that field because you knew you're gonna get some bad hops there.

When they opened Riverfront Stadium, I was happy just knowing we'd no longer have to play at Crosley Field. Crosley was like a gimmick stadium to me. To this day I don't understand why they had that incline in left field. As a left fielder, you'd fall down at least once in your career trying to get accustomed to it. I don't understand why they would do that or how the league would ever approve such a thing. Why didn't they make the field flat? I suppose if you played on it every day you might get used to it, but I don't know how guys like Tommy Harper, Deron Johnson, and even Pete Rose could have enjoyed it. I was glad to get out of here.

No matter what kind of fields that had come into the league, it seemed like they were giving the fielding awards to the same guys every year, especially at first base. There'd been only three guys to win the award in the National League since its inception in '57. Hodges won it the first three years, then Bill White of the St. Louis Cardinals won it seven straight times, and then it was Wes Parker's turn to dominate that category.

I committed only two errors all season long and had a better fielding percentage than Parker, but he won the award. Don't get me wrong; he was a great defender and maybe had a little more range than I had, but for the sake of argument, it could have been me. A lot of these things are won by people with reputations. Even the picking of the All-Star team. When the fans vote, it was all about popularity. A lot of guys didn't make the All-Star team because the fans picked their favorites early on. And then if they had a halfway decent season, they still got the vote over an unknown guy who might be hitting .350.

And I always caught with two hands. I wasn't fancy, and that may have looked boring to some, but I was consistent and had good hands and was in the right position, thanks to Hodges. I didn't want to miss a ball trying to be fancy or showing off. I'm sure it probably came down to Parker having almost 500 more chances than I had at first, and that makes some sense. I think if you're full time, and it's close between two guys that the guy playing every day should have the edge. But there were no minimum requirements for chances that I knew of. It wasn't like the batters needing so many plate appearances to qualify for the batting crown. I wasn't upset or anything like that. I was proud of my defense and knew I did a good job. It would have been nice to be recognized for it even once.

It also seemed apparent to me that we'd need some big boppers on the club to compete again for the division. We'd had the pitching to compete, but they started getting their share of injuries, and with our lack of a potent offense, you couldn't expect them to give up three runs or fewer every game. We didn't have that 30-home run, 100-RBI guy that teams ahead of us had. The Pirates had Willie Stargell and Roberto Clemente. The Chicago Cubs still had Ron Santo and Billy Williams. We didn't have one guy with over 14 home runs that year. Myself, Cleon Jones, and Tommie Agee had 14 each. Sure, Clendenon and myself combined for 25 in our platoon (and 95 RBIs), but none of the trades we were making were bringing over that one, 30-home run, All-Star kind of guy, a guy who played every day against righties and lefties. Someone you could slot in behind Jones.

The off-season dealing had only just begun when we shipped Art Shamsky, Jim Bibby, Rich Folkers, and Charlie Hudson to the St. Louis Cardinals for four other guys, none of which ever panned out. Shamsky was a good hitter and one of our heroes of '69. They were just trying to make something happen. They didn't know who to trade. Then, about two weeks later, they released Clendenon.

The release of Clendenon was another reminder for me that you never know what will happen. Here's a guy who came in a few years earlier who took my position, had a few good years while I went to the minors, and then to the bench, and, suddenly, he's released. Thinking back on it, I was really surprised that it hadn't been me who was traded or released, that for some reason I was still a New York Met.

And the Mets weren't done dealing. A few months later, they picked the wrong guy to trade, and we picked up former All-Star Jim Fregosi. I say former All-Star because when Fregosi came in he wasn't in shape when he came to spring training and never did get into shape. I didn't think he was capable of playing shortstop anymore, and he proved that during spring training. He wasn't a star anymore. So they put him at third where he could never figure it out. He struggled in '72, then was sold to the Texas Rangers the following year, opening the door for Wayne Garrett to get the hot-corner job, which he did admirably in '73.

It's hard for me to even say now, but not only did we give away Nolan Ryan in the Fregosi deal, also we dealt another promising outfielder name Leroy Stanton, who did pretty good with the California Angels and Seattle Mariners. Another four-for-one-deal that really ended up being the worst trade the Mets had made. You look at those trades in the '70s, and they mostly were horrible. We gave away Ryan, and he becomes a star. That was discouraging to watch him develop because we knew he had the best arm on the squad, just didn't get an opportunity. They didn't know what to do with him so they traded him. It was the same old Mets not doing their homework.

We always seemed to be a step behind when it came to trades involving the big-name players, but it seemed the Mets were thinking the same way I was thinking and traded for Rusty Staub just before the '72 season started, and that surprised me. With Shamsky gone, we all assumed the right-field job was Ken Singleton's, but in order to get Staub, we had to part ways with him. We gave away a lot by moving Singleton, Mike Jorgensen, and Tim Foli. It was hard to give up a good hitting switch-hitter not yet in his prime, but Singleton hadn't come close to putting up numbers like Staub was doing every year. Jorgensen didn't work out because he had that uppercut swing at a time when they frowned upon that unless you were a true power hitter, and he wasn't. He was good defensively, no question about it, but he never had a good season in his entire career. I don't think

Hodges took it out on Foli for the incident he had with me, but Buddy Harrelson had emerged as our every day shortstop, making him expendable. Staub was that pure hitter, All-Star player who played every day that we sorely needed. He'd made the All-Star team five straight years, could hit 30 and drive in 100, hit .300, could hit lefties as well as righties, and was never injured. In my book he hit all the checkmarks for the type of guy we needed.

But our minds weren't really centered on the trade. It was only a few days earlier when we got word that Hodges had died of a heart attack after playing golf with the coaches.

Of course, it was one of the saddest days I could remember, not only for losing our manager, but also losing a guy who'd taught me so much about the game and about being a man. He'd taught me all the little things I'd never known about playing first base, like utilizing the bag and proper feet positioning on taking throws coming from different angles. And he'd taught me how to be a man and take responsibility for myself. Ever since the Foli incident, we'd been on the same page. I really missed Hodges more than people realized because for the first time in a long time I had everything going for me. He was a great manager. He did everything you had to do to win. He knew when to make all the right moves and didn't care what anyone thought when he did. There's no doubt we would have won more pennants with him had he stayed alive.

I hated losing and didn't like baseball as much as I should have when we were losing. And that's really the reason Hodges was so important to us. He changed the whole culture of the organization from a losing, laughingstock of guys to a club that should be taken seriously. He took us from a losing-is-contagious attitude to a winning one. He changed the defeatist attitude we had halfway through the season into a whole different culture. He was one of those guys who had the charisma you need from your manager. He has to get the credit for that because he was the reason that the whole organization changed, and the players demeanor changed from a club that was accustomed to losing.

We played good baseball in that 1968 year. We didn't lose 100 games and we lost a lot of close games. When it came to '69, he didn't tolerate all the bullshit and kept reminding us how we lost all those close games, and that was the key to turning things around and doing something small to help the club win a close game. It took us a while to catch on, but before long, we started to win and win the close games. Once it got going, it steamrolled into a positive direction, and baseball was fun again. We all knew our roles, there was no fooling around, and we knew when we were gonna play and when someone was going in for defense. We were no longer playing lackadaisical but playing with purpose.

When I signed, I knew there was going to be an opportunity to play, and always being on championship teams, it was a very difficult adjustment to make mentally. I wasn't accustomed to that, and the atmosphere was so different from that. All of a sudden, everything changed when Hodges took over. That's called a leader. We now had a leader of your platoon. That was Gil Hodges.

I wish Hodges would have been our manager early on in my career because I needed someone like him to help me with the mental aspects of losing. You still want to perform for yourself because we were all on one-year contracts, but it wasn't easy to come prepared every day mentally as you should because you just know the outcome is gonna be the same. That's why so many guys wanted to leave because nothing good comes out of losing games, just more negative statistics.

So you learned to play for yourself at those times in the second half of the season, but that was still hard to do. After a while, the reporters brought up the same old shit that you're sick of hearing about it. I was young and immature with a lot of pressure put on me, and the publicity that we got all negative. You can say you're still out there for yourself, and as a kid you still want to play the game you love, but you're losing all the time. The game is the game, but that atmosphere around the game had to change, and it did when the Mets brought in Hodges.

I'm sure some of this may sound like I'm ungrateful or that I didn't like playing baseball, but that's not true. I think it's a lot like any competitive business. That no matter how hard you try, if you're always on the bottom looking up, after a while it's easy to get down on yourself. But our failures were public, and I understand all that with sports. And I'm grateful we had Hodges at a time when we needed him most. We entered that 1972 season, still shocked and dazed by Hodges' sudden death. The Mets replaced Hodges with Yogi Berra, which was popular with the fans but not so much with the ballclub.

It was a poor choice of managers. Berra was a great guy and socially he was everybody's friend. He wanted to be friends with everybody, but that's not what you're looking for out of your manager. Berra didn't have the sharpness or the strictness to be the manager. We went from Hodges' strict ways and his disciplinarian approach to Berra letting everybody do what they wanted to do, and soon enough, nobody's running the ship and that affected the ballclub's focus.

Under Hodges, you played good defense and fundamental offense like bunting, hit and run, taking the extra base. In the third inning, Hodges would be thinking about things that might happen in the seventh and eighth innings early in. Berra was thinking about what he should have done instead of what thinking of what he'd done earlier. He just wasn't as sharp, and we had no direction.

I think most of us wanted Whitey Herzog to replace Hodges. He was the most qualified guy who'd run the farm club during that time. Most of us had some interaction with him, and he'd help develop a lot of guys still on the roster. Most of us thought Herzog was the natural choice, but as usual, the Mets decided on the guy with the name. That decision didn't sit well with Herzog, and the Texas Rangers took notice, signing him as manager after the '72 season. With all that had happened with Hodges and the way the Berra hiring was done, we were still the players with no say on such matters. We knew we had to concentrate our efforts on playing the game and not to dwell on what could have been, so we vowed to play the season for Hodges.

It couldn't have been more scripted for such a thing to happen. We raced out to the best record in baseball (31–12), winning the close games like we had in '69 (the Mets had started the season going 10–0 in one run games), and Staub was proving that it was a good trade so far. He was our leading hitter, played a great right field, and with Berra's new lineup with him batting in the cleanup spot between Agee and Jones, it was the first time we'd had a power-hitting middle of the lineup like that one. And with expectations for Fregosi being the old Fregosi batting in the sixth spot, it was a formidable lineup to deal with and about to get better.

Joan Payson had always wanted Willie Mays back in New York, and she made it happen in May. He wasn't the marquee player in San Francisco like he once was, and the Giants had a few players in San Francisco that even the fans liked better, like Willie McCovey and Bobby Bonds. Mays was at the end of his career when we got him, but he was the still the premier player in baseball, and that's what Mrs. Payson saw, and we welcomed him when he got to New York.

And Mays was great on the field and off and great for the fans of New York. We knew it was mostly for public relations, that in his heyday you couldn't make a trade for Mays. We knew he was a shell of the player he once was, but he could do things to generate excitement. And he was willing to cooperate and helped the players. He offered his services and his office was always open, and you could always go over to him. And it was great to see all the attention he got visiting all the other cities when we arrived from out of town. There was tremendous excitement around that trade, and we needed something like that and we got it. He helped us.

But I was wondering where they'd put him in the field and in the lineup. I knew he was transitioning to first base, so that's where they put him for his first game with us as a leadoff hitter. It was so ironic that his first game was against the Giants, but when he homered in the fifth inning to break a 4–4 tie, it really felt like a script out of Hollywood.

But all the scripting and all the vows and dedications to win for Hodges all seemed to change the day Staub was hit by a pitch against the Atlanta Braves in early June. Staub attempted to play through the pain, but he wasn't the same guy after that. He played for another two weeks or so but had lost his power and you could see he was struggling with gripping the bat. He'd only missed seven games in the past four seasons, but after he went out, we fell apart.

And it wasn't just him. Jones missed a couple of weeks at the same time, and Agee missed about a month. Then one guy after the other went out with some sort of injury, opening up more playing time for the young John Milner and myself. When Staub did come back late in the season, it was too late to make a difference. We were out of the race.

Chapter 13

YOU GOTTA BELIEVE

WE'D BEEN THREE YEARS removed from our 1969 pennant-winning team, and it was clear the Pittsburgh Pirates were the kings of our division and would be the favorites again, going into '73. But a plane crash that killed Roberto Clemente on New Year's Eve took away a big part of the heart and soul of their team.

It was a tragedy for all of baseball to lose a man of his magnitude. A humanitarian working to aid a poor country ravaged by an earthquake suddenly taken in a tragic accident. As much as I knew how the world had lost a great person, I knew the Pirates would miss him like we'd missed Rusty Staub the year before. The Pirates didn't really do anything big in the off-season to help themselves, but we'd already traded Tommie Agee and Gary Gentry, picked up Felix Millan and George Stone, and by July had given up on Jim Fregosi and sold him to the Texas Rangers.

Agee wasn't performing like he did in the beginning, and I think they wanted to continue breaking up the organization. Agee had a good year, then a bad year, and that's the way baseball is sometimes. I should know. I'd come off a good '71 season only to see another big drop-off in production. But it was everybody. With all the injuries we had, Cleon Jones was the only guy with over 50 RBIs, and not one of us had 100 hits.

That 1973 season started out nothing like '72. We floundered around .500 for the better part of the season, then really hit the skids in July. We'd been swept at home by the Atlanta Braves to open a homestand, had fallen to last place and 12 games below .500 about a week earlier, and trailed the always fast-starting Chicago Cubs by 12.5 games. That's when Donald Grant, the team's chairman of the board, held a pregame team meeting to try to put a spark into us.

Of course, we knew what we'd done in '69 when we'd been in a similar position looking up at the Cubs. And it was fresh on our minds what we'd done in '72. But there wasn't just one club ahead of us in the standings like there was in '69. The whole division was ahead of us. And the injuries that kept happening were still happening. We had a lot of injuries, no question about it in '73, but we still didn't play the sound baseball that we were capable of.

So we gathered in the locker room, and Grant started talking about the '51 New York Giants overcoming the 13-game lead by the Brooklyn Dodgers, and that we were capable of doing the same thing, that some of our key players would be coming back from injuries. He was a businessman and rarely held a team meeting like this one, or even came into the clubhouse. But he thought it was important to talk to the team and not give up with so many games still to play. And so, in a very low-key voice, he was very stern and very serious, and when he talked, we listened.

Tug McGraw was an excitable character, but Grant didn't really know how excitable he was. McGraw always wanted to have a good time because every day was an adventure for him. Things didn't bother him like they did most players. We really didn't talk about negatives on the road. You really wanted to be a positive person, so we really didn't talk about struggles because we all were doing horseshit. He was a happy-go-lucky guy who liked pulling clubhouse pranks like lighting a guy's shoe on fire, laughing hysterically while watching the guy jump around the room. He would get mad at himself and bang his glove and do shit like that when things weren't going well, but he didn't rant or rave. He wasn't like Jerry Grote, who would leave the area and not talk to the reporters. McGraw wouldn't leave the locker area if the reporters wanted to talk to him. He stood right there and took the pressure and answered their questions.

And they had a lot of questions for him because he'd been one of the reasons why we'd been so far behind. In the last month alone, we'd lost six games in the other teams' last at-bat, and McGraw had two losses, several blown saves during and before that stretch of games, had just gotten blown out by the Braves. So if anybody should have been down on themselves listening to Grant giving a rah-rah speech, it was McGraw. But that wasn't his style. He was the same guy when things were going well or if he was pitching poorly. Down the stretch, McGraw really turned his season around and aside from us getting healthy at the same time and Jones carrying the offense down the stretch, McGraw was winning games and saving games just about every time he went out there (five wins, 12 saves in 19 appearances).

About halfway through Grant's speech, McGraw shouted out, "Let's go, we can do it," trying to agree with Grant's speech. I was standing right next to Grant and could see his expression changing and I could tell he thought McGraw was mocking him. I could see Grant staring at McGraw who kept shouting, "Let's Go Mets" and, "You gotta believe." When Grant ended his speech, he walked off in a huff outside the clubhouse. And I said to myself, *This doesn't look good.*

Before Grant made the turn around across the room toward the training room, I ran over to McGraw and told him he had to be careful with Grant. That I knew him for all these years, that he's a real businessman, and he looked a little pissed with all the yelling and screaming. I told McGraw that he inter-rupted him in the middle of his speech, and he took it as a sign of disrespect, that he jumped onto his rallying call before he finished. Well, McGraw said he didn't mean any of that, and I believed him. He said he didn't mean anything by it, so I told him he'd better go outside and tell him what you were trying to do, that you weren't mocking him at all. And so he did. I was McGraw's roommate and I didn't want to see him get traded over something like this, but I'd seen it before with Casey Stengel and Gil Hodges, so I knew it could happen. If you ever heard him talking at an event, he was into it and very high strung. He didn't care what he said.

I took him with me toward Grant and I said, "I want to introduce you to somebody, Mr. Grant. Tug, tell him what you said and why you said it." Right after that, Grant said he was glad McGraw came over and acknowledged him and that he thought he was playing games with him. They shook hands, and everything seemed to be okay. But I really thought he was gonna get traded right there. I'm pretty sure if I didn't step in, Grant would have taken that to the front office and negotiated a trade.

But it really took some time for that the war cry of McGraw's to really mean something. Everybody did start to get healthy, and we started to play better, but it didn't really show in our record. We hadn't moved out of last place into late August, and played right around .500 ball (26–24) since Grant's speech. There were only about 30 games left, we're 10 games below .500, we're looking up at the rest of the division that was suddenly the St. Louis Cardinals' to win.

They say you can't win your division in April, but you sure can lose it. I think the Cardinals proved that saying was true with the start they had (3–15 in April). But they'd come back strong and seized control of the division sometime in the middle of July. (From May 1–July 22, the Cardinals went 48–30, moving into first place) then they went into a slump, the Pirates got hot, and the Cubs had done their usual swan dive since another great start to the season. And we'd finally passed somebody in the standings, (the Philadelphia Phillies and the Montreal Expos) and even though we were still below .500 and hadn't been there since late May, we still had a chance despite our record. With the Cardinals leading the league with exactly a .500 record, it wasn't hard to believe the team coming out of the East could have a losing record. Some writers took advantage and wrote some stories of the unfairness of it all, pointing out the West had four teams with better records than any of us in the East, that whichever team came out of the West would have their way with the East winner. But you couldn't pay attention to all that. There'd been times before when two teams had 100 or more wins in the same year, so fair was fair. All we knew was we still had a chance and needed to get hot.

And I was in the same position I'd been before, playing mostly first base and a little left field. With John Milner being our other left first baseman/outfielder, they got us in together against righties because Jones was missing so many games from his injuries. In August they moved Willie Mays from the outfield to platoon with me at first base, so all in all, I was playing but not as much as I thought I would be after '72.

I hit a home run off of Juan Marichal in June, and that was it, my only one of the season. That's crazy to think back on that now. That in over 300 plate appearances, just one home run. Even Millan (three) and Don Hahn (two) had more than I did, and they were mostly singles hitters. I don't remember why that was. I don't remember having any nagging injuries that would have taken away some of my power and I don't remember thinking much about it. What I did know was with all our injuries, I was in the lineup as much as I was out of necessity, and had we been a healthy ballclub, it probably would have been the bench for me.

At the end of August, I knocked in a pair of runs late to beat the Cardinals in St. Louis that brought us out of last place for good, then drove in two more with a triple that helped us beat the Phillies. It was right around that time when we went into fourth place and when we made our move.

It was almost a repeat of the schedule we had down the stretch in '70 when we trailed the Pirates late in September and lost six of those seven games. It was a helpless feeling sitting on the bench and watching the whole thing unfold. But as bad as our record was at the moment (73–76), we knew we'd have to take four of the five games left with the Pirates to have a chance. But it wasn't just Pittsburgh we needed to pass in the standings. The Expos and Cardinals were barely ahead of us, and the Expos were on a decent winning streak.

The exciting thing about the schedule back then was that we played our own division the entire month of September, and that meant you had a chance if you did well against those teams. We couldn't afford to split or lose any series at this point. We needed to take three of four, two of three, or even sweep a series. But we hadn't done that all year long, and with the exception of the Pirates, had a losing record against our own division.

But none of that mattered. At the end of August and into the first few days of September, we split four with the Cardinals, then won four straight series against the Phillies, Expos, Phillies again, and the Cubs. We headed into Pittsburgh for two games. Then it would be back to Shea for three more against the same Pirates team. We lost the opener to the Pirates, then reeled off four straight wins against them. And incredibly, we went from being stuck in fourth or fifth place to the division lead.

We had Tom Seaver going, and Seaver was having a terrific season, but Yogi Berra pulled him after he a gave up a few home runs in three innings. That certainly wasn't the way to begin five games against the team you had to win four from, especially with our ace on the mound. We had our work cut out for us, but it felt like more of the same after we grabbed the lead on a single by Rusty Staub, and then they had a big inning and led going into the ninth. I don't recall a game all year where we'd trailed by three in the ninth and rallied to win. It just wasn't that kind of year like 1969 when everything fell into place with late rallies. But ever since Grant's meeting, McGraw reminded us we gotta believe, and there really was no better time to put his words into action.

Bob Moose was sailing along until they pulled him after giving up a few hits in the seventh. Yes, the same Moose who no-hit us in 1969. He wasn't one of those guys who completed a lot of his games. So it was no surprise when they went to the bullpen and brought in lefty Ramon Hernandez to face Staub and Milner with two men on and only one out. But after Staub singled to load the bases, Milner hit one back to the pitcher for an easy inning-ending double play.

I don't remember what I was feeling or what the mood of the ballclub was at that point, but opportunities like that one with the bases loaded in a key spot didn't come up too often, especially with one of our power guys like Milner at the plate. Maybe our luck had run out again, and maybe 1969 really was a season of miracles, a once-in-a-lifetime thing you were part of. We only had about 10 games to play after this one, an absolute must-win. We went into the ninth still trailing, and Berra sent in Jim Beauchamp to pinch hit for me. It had always been about the matchups when it came to me and so many other guys that batted left-handed, and this time was no different: the right-handed-hitting Beauchamp facing the lefty Hernandez. Beauchamp had been a decent pinch-hitter but hadn't had a hit in a while or played very much either. But he started a rally with a single, went to third on a double by Wayne Garrett, and both came home on a triple from Felix Millan. Then when Staub walked, they brought in Dave Giusti, and Berra countered with Ron Hodges as a pinch-hitter.

Hodges had been another one of those guys who played sparingly and was not used to pinch-hitting. I say that because it's difficult to come off the bench like he or Beauchamp did and produce something positive for the club. I know I struggled that year as a pinch-hitter and I know how hard it is trying to get a hit in that situation. It's not often you see two guys pinch-hitting back-to-back hits, especially in such a key spot, but Hodges singled in Millan, tying the game and sending Staub to third. They say good things come in threes, and I guess they proved that right when light-hitting Hahn singled in a pair giving us the unlikely lead. Hahn had been known for his good defense and had driven in hardly any runs at that point in the season, so when he came through like he did, I can honestly say it felt like 1969 again with so many guys participating in the winning of a game.

But the game wasn't over quite yet. Back-to-back walks by Bob Apodaca to start the Pirates' ninth inning forced Berra's hand so he brought in Buzz Capra. After a bunt moved runners to second and third and an infield grounder scored a run, Berra had Willie Stargell walked, then Richie Zisk walked, and Manny Sanguillen came up with the bases loaded and two outs.

Capra had his ups and downs all season like most of us had but had pitched better since the beginning of August. He'd given up a homer to Milt May the night before, but here he was centerstage with the bases loaded and us needing an out. It's hard getting out of any inning without giving up a few runs with four walks issued by your pitchers. We all knew it. We'd all seen it before. The old adage that a walk was as good as a hit went through my mind. But when Sanguillen flied to left to end the game, a collective sigh of relief came out of all of us. It was a huge swing of momentum after that win. Instead of being four-and-a-half games back, it was down to two and a half.

We came home to Shea, knowing we'd likely need to sweep the Pirates to have a chance at winning our division. It wasn't mathematically impossible had we taken two of three, but with how crazy close (one-and-a-half games) it was between us, the Pirates, the Expos, and Cardinals, there was something riding on every single game, and a sweep would likely mean we could control our own destiny.

We led most of the way in the first game, a close one until Jones put the icing on the cake with a three-run homer in the eighth. Jones hadn't been able to duplicate what he'd done in 1969, but he was still that clutch hitter we'd relied on so many times before. I'm convinced all the injuries took their toll on him, and that had he been healthy, he would have been right near the batting leaders every year, maybe even won a batting crown or two. To see him getting his stroke back right when we needed it was good news for us.

But we trailed three times the next night, rallying to tie the game in the sixth on a single by Jones, in the eighth on a single from Millan and an outfield error, and a clutch, ninth-inning pinch-hit from Duffy Dyer. It was one of those nail-biting types of games, a game in which we battled back just to take it into extra innings. But that game would later be called, "The ball off the wall" game and for very good reason. I don't remember seeing a ball hit off the top of the wall and spin back into play, but in a pennant race being as odd as it was, it happened.

Usually when a ball hits the top of the wall, its momentum continues going forward and over the wall for a home run, but Dave Augustine's long fly ball in the 13th inning popped off the wall over Jones in left with a different spin to it. In a crazy season made crazier, Jones played the ball perfectly, relayed it to Kenny

Boswell, who turned and threw a one hopper to Ron Hodges blocking the plate at home, nailing Zisk for the out. As is the case after a guy makes a great defensive play to end an inning, Hodges singled in the winning run that same inning, and we completed the sweep the next day, went into first place, and held off the rest of the division, clinching on the last day of the season.

Looking back on that game and the two before it, you look at the guys involved in those wins and wonder what they were thinking then, what they're thinking now, and you hope they know how significant those games were and how those contributions in those games made for such a difference in our season. We had no idea Capra would pitch to his final batter of the season to get that save, that this would be Beauchamp's final season of baseball, or that Dyer and Hahn would be traded in another year. That's baseball for you.

It was appropriate that we'd clinched against the Cubs because it reminded us all of '69, and we'd missed that feeling. Of all the teams still in the race, the Cubs were the team we worried about the least. They still had the top lineup in the division, and the new manager Whitey Lockman ran them out every day like Leo Durocher had for years, faltering down the stretch from the hot day games in Chicago.

We really got lucky winning the division, but as they say, sometimes you're better off being lucky than good. We won our division with the worst winning percentage of any team in the history of baseball. And being that I was on that '62 team that lost 120 games as the most in the history of modern-day baseball, this put me into some strange mix of history.

You can examine a season a million different ways and try to put your finger on the whys and the why nots. One run games. Injuries. Trades. Every team looks at all that. We'd become a team that was stuck on winning 80 some games a year, and

there was plenty to look at as to why. For me, the Mets for-
tunes started to fall apart after Johnny Murphy's death shortly
after the '69 series and especially after Gil Hodges' death in '72.
Of course, all the injuries and trades had the biggest impact on
all that, and though we somehow found ourselves in another
World Series, it didn't feel the same.

Our trades had mostly backfired. It was a good trade getting
Staub and then Millan and Stone from Atlanta. That trade was
good because Millan played well all year at second. Millan got
a lot of base hits and almost hit .300. He could bunt and move
over the runner and could do a lot of little things and was good
defensively. Stone never had another season like that, but he
certainly pitched great down the stretch.

Atlanta got Gentry who had an elbow problem. Back in those
days, they didn't know how to repair it properly so a guy could
continue his career. That's why guys retired like Sandy Koufax.
Gentry was never throwing the same after he had surgery. So
we made a good deal of trading players who were not gonna
help us and got two guys who did. Kenny Singleton had over
100 RBIs and was the reason the Expos were still in the race,
Amos Otis became an All-Star in Kansas City, playing in the
outfield where he belonged, and Nolan Ryan became a 20-game
winner for the California Angels and led the league in strikeouts
in '72 and '73. Fregosi had been sold to the Texas Rangers, so
that deal was really Ryan for nothing.

As much as all these bad deals being made by an incompetent
Bob Scheffing impacted our future, and Hodges' death may have
been the start of the Mets slide, we found ourselves in the playoff
against the Cincinnati Reds. They reminded me a lot of the '69
Baltimore Orioles with all their power hitters up and down the
lineup and guys like Pete Rose and Joe Morgan setting the table
for guys like Johnny Bench, Tony Perez, and others. And it was

no different from what it was in '69, when we went in as under-dogs against the Braves, and I was wondering if I'd be playing.

We lost Game 1 by the score of 2–1 on late homers from Rose and Bench, then evened the series behind Jon Matlack's shutout, came back to Shea, poured it on with a big 9–2 win, and lost Game 4 in extra innings. I hadn't even played to that point. In fact, the only time I left the bench was for the brawl that happened in Game 3 when Rose and Buddy Harrelson got into it at second base. When things finally settled down, Mets fans started throwing all kinds of things at Rose out in left field. It got so bad, they threatened the game to be a forfeit if the fans didn't start behaving. And being that we were up by seven runs, I think everybody took that threat seriously and finally did settle down.

Berra finally started me in left field for the deciding Game 5 game. I was pissed that I hadn't played at all, so it gave me special satisfaction when my first-inning single scored two to give us the early lead. I suppose by putting me in, that could have made Berra look like a genius, maybe even like Hodges. But Berra was a far cry from being either one. In my mind, it was Berra's decision to start Seaver over Stone in Game 6 of the 1973 World Series that triggered the demise of the Mets.

Berra got lucky in '73. He was a good guy but not a good manager. He didn't know what the hell was going on. Even in '72 we were still a good ballclub in contention, then we fell apart, partly because of some managerial decisions that mattered coming down the stretch. He made different moves in the close games that everyone questioned in '72. Maybe it's not fair to compare, but we had more confidence in Hodges as a leader and felt he would have made some different decisions than Berra did during those games where they really mattered. You couldn't say anything about his personality because everybody loved him.

But when the game was on the line, you wanted a manager that could help you.

We all felt we would have won in '73 if Hodges was the manager. He wouldn't have pitched Seaver on three days' rest in the sixth game of the World Series and wouldn't have buckled under any pressure from the press like Berra did. There was no reason for Berra to pitch Seaver. We were up, three games to two, and didn't have to win the sixth game. We had to win the seventh.

But Berra was weak that way and put Seaver in for Game 6. And Seaver was tired at this point of the season. He pitched a lot of innings and wasn't used to going on three days' rest. Seaver was a great competitor. If you asked him to take the ball, he's going to take the ball because he's a pro. But if you asked him on the side if he should pitch Game 6, he'd tell you the extra day's rest might matter. We had Stone who pitched great coming down the stretch. He won a lot of ball games for us in September and he may have been our best pitcher. And he didn't throw as many innings as Seaver. I'm sure he was pissed because he was originally scheduled to pitch Game 6 before Berra changed his mind.

Seaver wasn't his best in Game 6, and we lost. And now Berra's pitching decision really made no sense. He could have come back on Sunday with Seaver and used Matlack in relief if he needed him and chose Matlack over Stone to start Game 7. Matlack had a so-so season but had a good September and had pitched well in his two starts in the World Series. But we had our whole pitching staff ready to pitch and a fresh Stone. He should have pitched Stone because everything was falling right for Stone that year. How do you skip him? Stone was one of the heroes of that 1973 pitching staff. He was the guy that should have pitched, and we were confident we would have won if he pitched the sixth game. Berra was not mentally prepared to manage the important games. He wasn't the leader we needed. You could talk him out of keeping you out of the lineup if he was resting you or you were in a slump. He could be talked out of things because he wanted to be everybody's friend. He just couldn't be talked out of what seemed logical in pitching Stone. It went over his head. When Berra didn't play Stone, it was like putting a pin in a balloon. And once we lost Game 6, we could have gotten on the plane from Oakland and came home to New York because we were that devastated. By the time we came back to the ballpark for Game 7 on Sunday, we were down in the dumps. I know that sounds ludicrous, but that's how I think most of us felt. Of course, we knew we could still win Game 7 and that anything can happen in a single game.

It didn't help how I was feeling because Berra played me in just one game in the playoffs against the heavily favored Reds, and I responded with a single in my first at-bat that gave us the early lead. They had a bunch of lefty pitchers, but he couldn't even get me in to pinch hit in that extra inning loss in Game 4. After we won the series, I was pissed at Berra.

It also didn't help that the Oakland A's had lefties Vida Blue and Kenny Holtzman, but I didn't play against Catfish Hunter either and had three pinch-hitting appearances for the series. I was annoyed at Berra because I helped get him into the World Series. I understood that they'd gone with Milner at first base for his power, but I couldn't understand why I never had a real chance to hit lefties like they gave to Milner. I knew I'd struggled against Holtzman when he was with the Cubs, and Blue had become a pretty dominant pitcher, but before the series started, Staub was hurt, and some of us were pissed that Berra played him after that first game.

They chose to play Hahn in right and put Mays in center for Game 1. When Staub came back for the second game, Mays went in as a pinch-runner for Staub and back to center for the ninth inning. That ninth inning for Mays was a mirror of what was happening to the Mets. A lot has been written about Mays stumbling around trying to make a catch against a difficult sun in center field, and it was hard to watch. We all knew it wouldn't have happened in his prime, that he would have made all the plays like he always had. And the afternoon sun had been brutal on the outfielders from both teams. You could see guys struggling to find the ball, so it was no easy task to ask of any center fielder.

But what happened to Mays started well before that game. Mays wasn't keeping himself in top playing condition and was in the training room getting massages all the time. He wasn't physically conditioning himself to play, and if an older player doesn't exercise, you can't keep up like you once did. But when he could play and did play, he performed and did something. He still had shades of greatness, and you could just imagine how good he was every day during the prime of his career. There were given days you saw Mays do things that he used to do every day, and now he was doing it occasionally. But he was always in the clubhouse, never created a stir, or did anything to draw attention to himself. He helped us in '73, but with Mays being out there in those key situations where he couldn't perform like we knew he could, Berra should have taken him out for defensive purposes, not put him in. Another reason to have missed Hodges. That would be Mays's last game.

And a lot had been written about our club since '69, with a lot of circumstances chipping away at the dynasty we thought we had. We'd experienced what it felt like to be on top, and like Mays, how little by little it all started eroding away. We lost that chance of glory in '73, and like Mays, it was over for us.

Chapter 14

JAPAN, YOGI, AND JONES

I DIDN'T KNOW EXACTLY where the club was headed in '74, because I didn't have a good feel for it. I still had a bitter taste in my mouth to how things ended in '73, and it felt to me like a hangover was in the air. With John Milner coming into his own, I was no longer feeling confident I'd be a starter or a platoon player. But considering the health issues we'd experienced for four years, there'd be playing time at some point in the season.

Right from the start, we never got things going. Another Opening Day loss, a seven-game losing streak in April, and falling into the cellar for most of the season. By the All-Star break, it was the Philadelphia Phillies in the lead, and once again, the whole division was ahead of us. It's a hard task on a team to overcome the entire division like we did in '73. But we didn't have another locker room speech given to us by Donald Grant or a war cry from Tug McGraw. We didn't have the rest of the division playing .500 ball, and as the losses mounted and the months went by, it was clear that the fire was out on our season.

That was a hard pill to swallow for me. Just seeing those 91 losses next to our record was a bitter reminder of what once was, and because of that, the '74 season felt like the '64 season to me. Changes needed to be made to restore the team to its glory that felt so long ago.

When we played in '69, you couldn't wait to get to the ball-park, everybody was in a positive frame of mind. In the early years, I tell you, it got tougher and tougher every year you were there until we started to win. For me, in '74, it felt like I was about to get on that roller coaster again. Up and down, but mostly down. I was on a high when I signed my contract, then got to the major leagues where I was losing every day. Then we won in '69, stayed competitive for a few years, lost Gil Hodges, we won in '73, then we went straight down to the bottom again. It looked and felt like the same shit to me that we had in the early years, and even though I hadn't reached 30, I felt like I was too old to accept it again.

And I was right about my playing time. For the third year in a row, I had fewer plate appearances than the year before, had fewer starts, and found myself more in a pinch-hitting role. A role that really started the year before. And despite all the troubles we had in winning games and my lack of playing time, I felt like I was finally coming into my own as a hitter, that I'd caught up to the league, and was seeing the ball better than I had in recent years. I think you become smarter as you mature and you look for certain pitches in certain situations. That's the mental preparation of baseball, and you don't know how to do that when you're 17. It's not a case that you walk into the major leagues and make all these adjustments right away. The pitchers are smarter than you; they control things because they have the baseball. They knew early on I was a fastball hitter, so they're not gonna throw me many of what I like. Next thing I knew, I had problems making adjustments, and I didn't adjust fast enough.

I didn't really see myself as a pinch-hitting specialist because I wanted to play every day still. And I didn't like pinch-hitting. I found it difficult to come off the bench cold at the end of games, but also knew it was a good time to make a point to try to get back into the lineup. But I struggled with the role and I knew it. I think I hit around .190 as a pinch-hitter before '74, (.188), and that's not helping your ballclub out when they needed it.

So I started to prepare myself to pinch hit during certain games, anticipating like a manager would, several innings in advance. I knew who was in the pen and who was on our bench and I'd go underneath behind the dugout and start warming up with some swings, trying to visualize a certain guy who might be coming in. As the season wore on, that strategy seemed to be working for me. There was a stretch of six games in July when I had a pinch-hit in five games and a walk in the other. I went to the plate with more confidence than I'd felt in years, and the fans had started chanting, "Eddie, Eddie" when I came to the plate. It was exciting for me. My average was right at .400. The fans were going crazy when I came to bat, but the only thing missing was the wins.

I got some more playing time, was still getting my pinch-hits, but the average dropped to around .300 by September. It was a lousy feeling that the club was really out of the race for the first time in years, but for the first time in my career this late in the season, I felt like I could finish at .300. I wasn't thinking about any pinch-hitting records because I don't recall any of that being brought to my attention. I wanted to bat .300.

I hit a slump that brought me down to .294, then went 3-for-4 against the Phillies, bringing me back above the line. With my average at .301 and my pinch-hitting average at .500, I pinch hit on the last game of the season, a ground-out in the ninth inning, leaving my final average at exactly .300 and my pinch-hitting average at .486—a major league all-time high that still stands today.

I was proud of that season because that was a magical year for me personally. It seemed like every time I got up to pinch hit I was hitting a hard line drive somewhere, and that was usually against a better pitcher. And aside from batting .300 and making a name for myself in baseball history, I collected my 1,000th major league hit, which came off of Steve Stone in May.

Aside from my personal achievements, the season didn't end for us in October. They'd asked the New Yorks Mets to play a barnstorming tour against some of the Japan teams following the '73 World Series, but there wasn't enough time for us to go. So they delayed the trip to the off-season of '74 instead.

The Mets were a known team in Japan, and a lot of the Japanese people knew about star players. But not all the Mets were willing to go. Cleon Jones was nursing an injury, Buddy Harrelson and Jerry Grote stayed back, and a few other guys stayed home. I think when that '73 series ended, a lot of the players were pissed that we pitched the wrong guy in Game 6. We'd all agreed to go the year earlier, but some guys were still mad at Yogi Berra for how he managed against the Oakland A's and didn't care how he felt about it.

When we got over there before the first game in Japan, I didn't play in it, so I brought it to Berra's attention that he hadn't played me in the World Series and now this. He said since so many of our veteran guys decided not to come that he was gonna use that trip to Japan as a proving ground for some of our young players to prepare for the next season. I was one of the few name players over there, so I got pissed off and told him I was going home if he didn't play me every day. He got upset and said I couldn't go home because the club had collected all of our passports when we landed. But I didn't hand mine in. I pulled out my passport and flashed it in front of his face and said, "I'm leaving tomorrow if I don't play." I stood my ground, and he knew I wasn't bluffing. That was the start of the demise of Berra. None of us respected him, and he was on thin ice.

So he played me every day, and we went 9–7 the next three weeks against some of their best teams. We went all throughout Japan, and they packed the stadiums with 50,000 at every game. They didn't throw as hard as our league and weren't so intimidating, but they had good control. Defensively, they worked their asses off and didn't fool around. If one of their starters got knocked out early, they sent him down to the bullpen where he continued to throw as a sign of manhood and continued pitching deep into the game. They didn't get the day off like they do here. They have a different concept on performance and are very dedicated. If a guy doesn't lay down a good bunt when he's supposed to, he's out there the next day practicing bunting for an hour. If someone makes an error, that guy's coming in early to work on it with 100 ground balls or so. And the players had to pick up their own equipment after the games. You could see that they had good players over there.

We played all Japanese guys and no American players. And they wanted guys. They asked me if I wanted to come to Japan when I retired, but I didn't like the conditions. It's not as upscale as it is in the states, and being by yourself as one or two Americans on a team with a language barrier had to be a problem. They had cities with nice ballparks, but I didn't want to be involved in that. They were trying to create goodwill, and it was fun, but our wives left early as it wasn't a true vacation for them. And the expenses were really high.

The team gave us money to use, but it was so expensive that we spent it all early.

In early November, Hank Aaron showed up as the ambassador of a home run hitting contest between himself and the all-time Japanese home run king, Sadaharu Oh. The Japanese fans loved the home run contest, and this was one for the ages. Aaron came over with just his uniform, so he needed a bat. He looked into our batting rack and he pulled a few bats out and he liked my model, which was similar to what he had. I think his handle was slightly thinner than my model, but it was the right weight and length, so he used it for the contest. My bat was 34 ounces, and that's heavy compared to today's bats. I had a K55 model, which had a thicker handle, and then I used the thinner handle R43 in the second half of my career. I was honored to know that the bat measured up to his liking. He didn't ask me if he could use it, but you're not gonna say no anyway to Aaron. It was more fun seeing the guy using my bat because he could have used any bat from that rack. Not that it means anything, it wasn't gonna make me into a home run hitter. But, don't I wish! He won the home run contest 10–9, and I had him sign it and he wrote on it his name and the date and what the occasion was.

As our games in Japan continued, I was hitting home runs with regularity, and so was Oh. In fact, we were tied for the most home runs by a player going into the final game against each other's team, and the MVP prize was on the line, a Kobe bull they'd lined up back by the backstop between the two dugouts.

So I hit a home run in the first inning, and they moved the bull closer to our dugout as if I now had the advantage of winning it. Now I figured I was gonna win the bull, but an inning or two later, Oh hit a home run, and they inched the bull toward his dugout. Later in the game, I hit another home run, and they moved the bull back to our side, where it stayed when the game ends. So they presented me with this fucking bull on the field at the pitcher's mound. Berra was out there with me and started taking these goddamn pictures like it's a big deal, as the damn thing was rearing up like he doesn't want me to be its new owner.

But I had no interest in taking this bull back home. I wanted to get home ASAP. They had originally left seven days for rain-outs on the schedule, but we hadn't had one, and when I asked if they could move the itinerary up so all could leave early and not have to stay another week, we were told it couldn't be done. Being the players' representative, I went to the ballclub because everybody wanted to leave and I asked them if the Japanese could move up our flight, but they refused to do that, forcing us to stay in Tokyo another week and pissing off more of the players.

So I had this big bull as a prize and I asked if anyone wanted to trade for my bull for a plane ticket home to New York. I don't recall if it was a fan or a player, but some guy jumped at the chance, and I got two first-class tickets home for the bull. I probably got beat on the deal because Kobe beef was probably worth a lot more money than two tickets, but I didn't give a shit. I couldn't get it home to New York. What was I gonna do with a bull? So I traded it to leave seven days early. That was another thing I did to Berra. I left the ballclub in Japan. I wanted to get home after being there for so long. I told him I was on my own time, and now he was pissed off.

With the trip to Japan, it was a short winter before spring training began. But I was anxious to get back to work and try putting '74 behind us. And as usual, we had some new faces and peddled some old friends away.

They'd traded Kenny Boswell and McGraw in December, two more guys from that special '69 club. Boswell was a good teammate and a good player, but his playing time and numbers were going down, and as hard as it was to see McGraw go, he'd had two below par seasons in a row, and no one from the bullpen had claimed the closer's role. When Ron Swoboda got traded and then McGraw, that was hard for me to take. Swoboda and I were very close, and it was too bad the three of us couldn't room together. That's how close we all were. When Swoboda got traded, I roomed with McGraw. When you grow up with somebody and have known them for so long, you hate to see them leave, and that's what happened during my career—until finally I was left there alone looking around, and nobody was in the room.

We'd picked up two more big names in the off-season, Joe Torre and Dave Kingman, and added a good outfielder in Del Unser. We'd been trying to get Torre for some time and, of course, we got him at the tail end of his career when his numbers were trending down. Kingman was a guy who could give us some much needed power in the middle of the lineup and the biggest power threat since Frank Thomas in '62. Kingman hit a bunch of home runs for us, mostly the moonshot variety that had the fans jaws dropping by the height and distance he hit them.

He ended up moving around quite a bit, but I think that was more because of his personality. What you saw with Kingman was a guy hitting tremendous home runs; he had more power than anybody. That was the good side of Kingman. But once you got him into the clubhouse, you saw a different side that was very self-centered in thinking about himself. He did himself a disservice with his attitude because even at the end of his career (35 home runs for Oakland in '86) he should have continued to play. That's not normal to go from having 35 home runs to not having a job. Torre was still a good hitter but past his prime. He joined us in Japan and did well, and when McGraw got traded, we became roommates.

But I had really found my stride and had the best average of my career, finishing at .323 to lead the club in that department. I didn't have nearly enough plate appearances to qualify for the batting title, but .323 still slotted into the sixth spot in my mind. I did have more playing time and I carried over my pinch-hitting abilities to be one of the league leaders in that department again. With two straight years of .300 batting, I felt like I was just getting started.

At least the season trended back up instead of down. We finished above .500 but fell apart down the stretch with a terrible September. Kingman did what he came over for and broke Thomas' single-season Mets' home run record (36), and for the first time in Mets history, a guy went over 100 RBIs (Staub/105), Unser played every day in center and almost hit .300 (.294), and Tom Seaver won his third Cy Young Award. But for all the good numbers that these guys produced, it was Mike Vail who became the latest young player to make a splash with the Mets.

Vail joined the club in August after a great season in Tidewater, where he led the league in hitting (.342) and would later be named International League MVP. We'd picked him up in a trade with the St. Louis Cardinals, but the Mets were always moving guys around from the minors, so to us, he was just another name. And guys with good minor league credentials didn't always pan out. By the time the Mets waived him in '78, that proved to be one of the best Mets trades in a franchise that made lousy deals. He was hot right from the start. We had a three-game series in San Diego where the

Padres couldn't get him out. I don't recall exactly what he did (9-for-14), but he was impressive. And he kept going after that, getting one or two hits in every game. As the hits kept coming, it was brought out by the press that Vail was within striking range of the rookie record of 23 straight games with at least one hit—set by former Met Richie Ashburn. He tied the record at home against the Expos.

It was great for Vail and great for the club to get noticed like that. He seemed like the real deal to me, but so did Amos Otis and Ken Singleton, so I was optimistic and leery at the same time, wondering what we'd do with him if things started going the other way, or if he had a prolonged slump. It was just the Mets way. But what I'd also noticed during that homestead were the small crowds, crowds that used to be 30 or 40,000 were now under 10,000. With crowds like that in a stadium holding 55,000, it felt more like being in the old Polo Grounds again.

Of course, there were other reasons why Vail became our left fielder. Jones had held down that position for years, and when he was healthy, he usually played there. But he'd been arrested in May while rehabbing in Florida, where the police said he was sleeping nude in a van parked on the side of the road with a nude, White woman with him.

They brought Jones home, assuming he was guilty as charged, then Grant ran Jones in front of the press to apologize. There were some incidences that involved Jones, like the day Hodges pulled him out from left field against Houston in '69, but this one was way different. This was not an easy thing to handle, but the Mets certainly handled it in an uncalled-for-way from a public relations standpoint. They embarrassed Jones and his wife, Angela. During the press conference, they said some demeaning things about Jones, and nobody liked that, then

Jones read from a prepared statement that he shouldn't have had to do. And that was the worst incident for me because even as the player representative, what could I say? I couldn't get involved in it. That could have created a bigger problem in the clubhouse. We all discussed how it was handled and all we could do to help him was to be his friend and teammate. But Jones took the high road, and I believe he became even a better person for it.

You certainly want to protect your players if they make a mistake, and the players thought the way they handled the van incident was a disgrace. Joe McDonald was a disgrace with the way he handled that situation, and I think he controlled the press conference. Then a couple of years later, there was a big article about him getting drunk in the middle of the night in the same town. And nobody said anything.

When Jones came back from rehab, he wasn't playing every day like he'd been used to his whole career. Milner was in against righties, and Berra even used Gene Clines a few times over Jones, so maybe Jones wasn't onboard with all that. I knew how he must have felt. I'd spent my whole career fighting for playing time, and now Kingman had shifted over to first base most games. That all came to a head in a game against the Atlanta Braves in mid-July when Berra brought in Jones to pinch hit for me. You could feel the tension brewing as Jones took his time getting ready. He lined out to short, and when the inning ended, he got into it with Berra.

Berra had told Jones to replace Kingman in left, but Jones refused to go, saying his knee needed to be wrapped to play defense. Jones shouted at Berra and stormed off to the clubhouse. I'd seen Berra upset a few times but not this angry. After the game Berra demanded that the club trade or release Jones, or Berra was gonna quit. They held a meeting that all parties attending, and for some reason, Berra's wife was there. Just another odd thing we never saw before. They tried trading Jones, he vetoed the trade, and they released him shortly after that. But what goes around comes around. Berra was fired two weeks later.

Chapter 15

THE BLUNDER YEARS: GOOD-BYE TOM TERRIFIC

THE USUAL OFF-SEASON FOR THE NEW YORK METS was a bunch of wheeling and dealing, and this one was no different. And as usual, the big trade was one I certainly didn't endorse. As the player representative, it wasn't my responsibility to talk to management about trades. My job was taking care of the players' issues in the clubhouse. As far as evaluating talent, you had no say in that at all, even when you knew you could do a better job yourself or make suggestions to help the ballclub. Anything that went on with the ballclub I could complain about, and it irritated me with most of the moves they made.

When they announced that the proposed Rusty Staub trade to the Detroit Tigers finally was made, I thought it was another huge blow to our present and to our future. Everyone knew we needed another stud starting pitcher, but Mickey Lolich was on the downside of his career, not in his prime. He'd still been the ace of the Tigers' staff but had a couple bad seasons pitching for a bad team. But the Mets were counting on him being the guy he was in the late '60s. It felt no different to me than when we acquired Warren Spahn at the end of his career, another star lefty hanging on. And look where that went. And Staub had become a fan favorite and just driven in 100 runs for us, played a great right field, and was consistently good.

I let all that sink in and took another look at the deal. Maybe the Mets weren't done dealing. With Cleon Jones gone, they'd probably keep John Milner in left, move Dave Kingman to right, and keep Del Unser in center. With Joe Torre in the mix somewhere, it looked to me like I could be getting more playing time as long as they didn't make any more trades. I had some time to think about it but found myself also thinking about our owner, Joan Payson, who died a few months earlier.

I'd been very close to Mrs. Payson since the day I signed, and as long as she was still in charge, I always thought I had a future with the club after my playing days were over. At the time, her death wasn't as devastating to the organization or to me personally as Gil Hodges' death was, but I'd find out in time that it should have been. Soon after she died, her husband, Charles, inherited her stake in the team. But Mr. Payson had no interest in baseball and handed the reins over to daughter Lorinda de Roulet, who was promptly put in charge of the club.

It was probably the worst timing for such a thing to happen. Joe McDonald had proven time and time again how incompetent he was with trades and signings, and then de Roulet took over the ballclub and she knew nothing of the sport. It had all the makings of the blind leading the blind. And I was right. We became the laughingstock of baseball. Strike one.

It was certainly a crucial time for the Mets. The New York Yankees had become the new darlings of the town. Attendance was down again and with what happened with Jones and Yogi Berra and the unpopular trade of Staub, it looked to be another turning point. And with free agency at its beginnings and teams trying to figure that all out, it was important to have the right people in place to understand the rules. Strike two. But strike three didn't come yet. We had a good season in '76 but were never in the race. I was right about the defensive alignment and played a lot more than I had the previous four years and almost hit .300 again. And I was right about Lolich. He had another losing season in his one year with us, then signed with the San Diego Padres, then out of baseball. What I didn't see coming was peddling Unser and Wayne Garrett to the Montreal Expos for a couple more guys who didn't help us. Thinking back on it now, it probably had everything to do with money. Speaking of money, Joe Frazier became our third manager in two years and was put into that position because the Mets didn't want to pay a lot of money to a manager. He was a nice guy, but we still needed that Hodges-type manager to run the club.

By now I'd seen enough and started thinking I'd be the right person for a front-office job, someone who evaluates talent and makes deals. I knew I could do a better job than they could and familiarized myself with the list of available free agents coming out. I knew who could help the ballclub and who they should pass on. And I also knew the club started to struggle financially and probably couldn't afford the big names.

I'd picked up some vibes from playing first base all these years and talking to the guys leading off, I had a good feel for which guys would be able to handle New York and the constant pressure from the press, something I didn't feel they paid enough attention to over the years with some of the trades they'd made. I was a friendly person and liked to talk to the guys when I was holding them on. You might just get a couple of words in because normally we didn't socialize with the opposing teams. They were the enemy. That was the concept and the mind-set. But I paid attention to the personalities.

New York can be a tough city, and I know because I grew up there. But when you're here as a player, there's plenty of press with guys from plenty of newspapers. I think when a guy like Jim Fregosi came here after being in California, there's some culture shock to it, especially if you underperform like he did. Handling the press in New York was very difficult. Fortunately, for me, I did pretty well with that. I was honest and straightforward and answered their questions. But some guys can't make that adjustment when they come to New York, and they get themselves in trouble by either not talking to the press or saying the wrong things. Those kinds of things can ruin careers.

But there were so many other opportunities for star players coming to New York, especially if we started winning again. After we won the Series in '69, tons of doors opened up for us. Rod Gaspar, Garrett, and Ken Boswell appeared as contestants on *The Dating Game* a few months after the season ended. We were on *The Ed Sullivan Show* as a group singing "You Gotta Have Heart," appeared on *The Merv Griffin Show, That Regis Philbin Show*, and a couple of movies used our names. I had a contract with Gillette shaving cream, appeared with Art Shamsky on *Sesame Street*; that was one of my favorites. We did the counting segments for young kids and we loved it. I became very popular in my neighborhood, not as Ed Kranepool from the Mets, but as Big Bird's friend. Every kid that came to my house wanted to meet Big Bird. It was great to see a little kid looking up to you as Big Bird's friend. We counted one to 10 and 11 to 20. They ran those segments for years.

But I didn't know if the Mets were shrewd enough or market-savvy enough to use opportunities like we were given to lure in new players. These were perfect examples of the things that did happen and could happen to a player in New York, something they should have stressed. But I'd put all that on the back burner for now. I was still only 31 and hitting better than I ever had. We had a good season, but finished a mile behind the Philadelphia

Phillies, and they were good. With guys like Mike Schmidt, Greg Luzinski, and a great pitching staff, we couldn't compete with them on paper. And they'd be coming back with something to prove after losing to the Cincinnati Reds in the playoffs. We needed to see where we went with the new class of free agents.

There were some big names on the list of free agents, but our big signing was former teammate Ray Sadecki. Sadecki had pitched well for us in the past, but, like Spahn and Lolich, he was at the end and was cut in early May. We should have gone after two other lefty starters, Mike Cuellar or Don Gullett, but Cuellar signed with the California Angels and Gullett with the Yankees, the big spenders in the free agency signings. So we started off bad in '77. Real bad. And after a six-game losing streak at the end of May, we found ourselves in last place, our (15–30) record the worst in baseball. So they fired Joe Frazier and replaced him with Joe Torre. Frazier met with Donald Grant and Torre at Grant's Wall Street office where he made the changes in person. I'm sure that was awkward for both Joes, being replaced as a manager by one of your players sitting next to you. They say he handled it well.

But I had my own problems to deal with before the season began. I had my own meeting with McDonald, and he offered me a three-year deal. I thought it was a fair deal and asked him if I could go home, discuss it with my wife, and call him in the morning. That seemed to be a fair enough request to make on my part, so we shook hands, and I drove myself home. It was a fairly short drive home, but when I arrived home, my wife said McDonald had called. So I called him back, and he said he rescinded the offer.

So I went over to see Grant about it and told him what had happened. McDonald was the general manager of the ballclub, but we knew Grant made most of these types of decisions. Grant told McDonald that I was in the office with him, and that I'd told him what happened with him rescinding the offer, and wanted to know if that was true. He told him it was, and Grant told him he can't do that to a player. Then he asked him what the amount of the offer was. Before they got off the phone with each other, Grant told McDonald to tear up the contract and write out a new one for $10,000 more per season. Of course, that made McDonald look bad and probably came back to haunt me later on. He was still the GM and probably was pretty ticked off about what had just happened.

But they were two different guys. McDonald would come into the dugout and look up at our names above our lockers so he could remember who we were. Grant would shake your hand and start a conversation with you. And Grant was taking all the heat and flack about the club from the press, but the personnel decisions were being made by McDonald. I even asked him at our meeting why he was allowing that to happen, why he wasn't defending himself. But he brushed it off and paid attention to my issue.

Meanwhile, the Mets were in another public relations disaster with the way they were handling Tom Seaver's contract. Seaver had originally agreed to a new contract but then asked for it to be torn up and renegotiated. There were some bitter articles written about Seaver by Dick Young, and they even started writing negative things about his wife, Nancy. And as hard to believe as it was, it looked like our franchise player was gonna be traded.

I was Torre's roommate, so I was privy to whatever he wanted to tell me. I used to sit next to Torre during the games and really was his confidant. He'd talk to me about potential trades, especially the one that was brewing with the Los Angeles Dodgers and asked me to come up with six guys from a list of guys the Dodgers were willing to trade. So I made a list of six guys, and he had his list, and it was the same six guys, full of guys that could help us now. So Torre went out early to the ballpark the next day to present his list to McDonald, but in typical McDonald fashion, he negotiated a trade with the Reds in the middle of the night. Torre wasn't even in on the trade. He had no idea the trade had been made.

So Torre was pissed they made the trade and he wasn't even part of the negotiations. And that created a major thing in the clubhouse. That was a major, major thing after we read the names of the guys we'd traded for. Both Torre and I were upset because we knew the Dodgers players would have made us a better club than what we got from the Reds. I don't remember the entire list, but three guys I remember we would have been Pedro Guerrero, Rick Rhoden, and Lee Lacy. All those Dodgers became really good players. Guerrero and Lacy became .300 hitters. Rhoden was a solid starter. But McDonald was probably drunk when he made the deal, and nobody said anything about the shit that he did. He was also the one who embarrassed Jones in front of the press, so he'd made a habit of screwing things up.

We got a bunch of names in the deal, and the ballclub immediately gave all of them long-term contracts. Free agency was a new thing, so teams wanted to keep guys around for a while. But that made no sense to me either. Hardly anybody that we had stayed around for five years. They just kept trading guys away. The new guys all got hefty contracts, and I thought it was quite strange giving players who hadn't even tested the system and giving five-year guaranteed contracts when you're in last place.

Deep down, I was kind of annoyed at that point because we had played so many years for them on one-year contracts. Why give them big money, more than anyone else was getting, and we're in last place? It didn't make any sense to us. That was another part of the demise of the Mets because they slid down very quickly after that. Guys became complacent and didn't perform, and we certainly weren't an exciting ballclub. What we got in return for Seaver in Doug Flynn, Steve Henderson, Dan Norman, and Pat Zachry didn't justify the trade for Seaver.

The thing about Seaver was that he was so smart on the mound. He knew that Henry Aaron was not gonna beat him in the ninth inning. He might walk Aaron and give him nothing good to hit, knowing he still had to face a guy like Orlando Cepeda, who was another great hitter. But he wouldn't give Aaron a fastball down the middle. He had a strategy for every pitch and for every hitter. He had a great arsenal of pitches, but he knew how and when to use them. And it was rare that a Henry Aaron or an Orlando Cepeda even beat him in the ninth inning.

To make matters worse, we traded Kingman that same day and got a utility player and reliever back in the trade. I think trading Kingman kind of got lost in the shuffle that day. That was like another big surprise that hadn't been talked about. People were so concerned about Seaver and who we were gonna get for him, so nobody was really thinking about Kingman being traded. Everybody knew something was going on with Seaver, and then suddenly both trades go down. On the same day, we lose our best pitcher and top slugger. It was hard to process. Strike three.

That was really the final dagger of the many turning points to the Mets downfall when we traded Seaver. The whole organization, except McDonald, was stunned when that trade came about. We certainly needed something positive, because everything surrounding us seemed so negative, but this trade wasn't it. We were going in the wrong direction with terrible leadership making one terrible decision after the other. I still enjoyed playing for the Mets, but you still wanted to win and contribute, but we traded Seaver and Kingman the same day, breaking up the ballclub with some quality veterans. That's the discouraging thing about playing for an organization that gives away the wrong players. They stockpiled many players who played the same position. I never cared where I played. I just wanted to play.

But it didn't matter that I was hitting .300 again. I was on my way to 500 at-bats, but I could see I was gonna be the odd man out again. I saw who we got in return for Seaver and knew that I wasn't gonna play. Once you trade a Seaver, you have to justify the trade, and Henderson was the one guy they sent over who they thought was gonna be a superstar. I knew the outfield alignment would be Henderson, Mike Vail, and another rising star in Lee Mazzilli. They'd take Milner out of left field for good and leave him at first base. And with a good hitter like Bruce Boisclair pining for and deserving to play, they needed him somewhere in the mix.

But the long season had always provided opportunities to play. We'd always had so many guys with injuries or guys going into slumps, like what happened to Vail. Here was a guy we all thought was gonna be a .300 hitter, and after his rookie year, when he had that 23-game hitting streak, he dislocated his foot playing basketball and didn't join the club until late in the season. He struggled that year but came back strong and was hitting about .360 when the Seaver trade was made. They kept him in right until he hit a big slump and started sharing outfield duties with Boisclair. Buddy Harrelson was still our shortstop, and Felix Millan was our second baseman, but they wanted to get Flynn plenty of playing time, so they moved him around all the time between second, short, third, you name it.

Injuries are always happening in the game, and you expect guys to recover from most of them. But the injury that happened to Millan in August was the end of his career, a body slam by Pirates catcher Ed Ott during a routine play at second. Ott came in hard at second, trying to break up a double play, probably a little too hard, and the next thing you know, Millan took a swing at him, and Ott picked him up and slammed him to the ground. Both benches emptied, but nothing came of that. They had to bring a stretcher out on the field, and later, when they announced the results, Millan had suffered a crushed shoulder, an injury he never recovered from. That injury gave more playing time to guys like Joel Youngblood and kept Flynn in the lineup for good. But with Henderson showing that he had the potential to be a star, and Mazzilli having a great season and Milner still at first, nothing opened up for me. I got my starts but really started back into my pinch-hitting role. I didn't get the same batting average when I broke the pinch-hitting record in '74 (.486), but I wasn't far off (.448) with another great season.

At the trading deadline, they dealt Jerry Grote to the Dodgers, another important guy from that '69 club. Grote was a hard-nosed guy in every way—on the field and in the clubhouse. I'm sure over the course of his career he'd alienated a lot of umpires because he was tough to play with and against. I dressed alongside of him for 10 years and didn't even want to say hello to him in the morning. He'd get you in a bad mood sometimes. Once he got in the range of the ballpark, I think his mood would change. I guess it was his way of preparing himself for the game, but he was a very tough competitor. If an inning ended with a strikeout and the ball was in his hands, he'd roll it as far away from the mound as he could as a sign of disrespect for the other pitcher. He was a guy you definitely wanted on your team.

Grote was known mostly for his defense, but he had so many clutch hits for us during that '69 season. He was one of our key guys that was injured early in '73, and when he and a few other guys came back off of injuries, that's when we started winning. I was happy for him that he went to the Dodgers and played in another World Series that year and the following year. He had talked about retiring after the '77 season, but I guess playing on a winning team helped change his mind.

When it finally came to an end, there wasn't much good to say about the '77 season. The Seaver trade. The Kingman trade. Grote gone. Millan's injury. Bad press. Horrible attendance. There were games at the end of the season with crowds smaller than what we had at the Polo Grounds, three to four thousand if we were lucky. With the Yankees winning like they were, the whole thing flipped, and they were the darlings of New York again. We were a bad team. If it hadn't been for a couple of wins in St. Louis at the end, we would have lost 100 games, and that brought back some bad memories. It really was the early Mets for me again. I had come full circle.

Thinking back on that season, I think the blackout game we played against the Cubs in July, when the lights literally went out in the sixth inning and stayed out in New York for a day, couldn't have been more appropriate timing to our season, or to an extent, what had happened to the Mets rise and fall. I'm not a big believer in such things. Well, at least I wasn't back then. But now that I've had time to think about such things, when the stadium went dark, it may have marked the end of an era. Lenny Randle was in the batter's box when the lights went off, and he thought his life had just ended. That statement Randle made may have been personal, but it really was more of a reflection on the '77 Mets. It was over.

Chapter 16

END OF THE LINE

I DIDN'T MISS A DAY OF PLAYING in all those years because of an injury and I wasn't out for a cold or the flu or anything like that. I started having some foot issues with my bunions, so at the end of that '77 season, Joe Torre asked me to get my bunions removed and promised me I'd be playing every day in '78. So I had the surgery, and the surgery went fine, and by all reports, I'd be ready to go for spring training.

Then in December, the New York Mets made another big splash in the trade market. A colossal, four-team trade involving about a dozen guys. When it was all said and done, John Milner and Jon Matlack were gone, and in return we received another past his prime, part-time outfielders in Ken Henderson and in Tom Grieve and a flamboyant first baseman by the name of Willie Montanez.

They were always looking for more offense, but starting pitchers—especially lefties—were always at a premium. Matlack had an off year in '77, but a lot of the great pitchers had off years, and he was just getting into his prime. Milner had an off year as well, but who didn't? Maybe the front office just wanted to make some changes for the sake of making changes. After the trades were made, they said they were rebuilding, that there were enough arms in the system to justify the Matlack trade. That made no sense to me. They traded away a proven pitcher and were banking on some of the young guys coming up. Maybe they thought we'd have a repeat of when Tom Seaver, Jerry Koosman, and Nolan Ryan came up at the same time. But we all knew those things were rare to happen. We should have hung on to Matlack and let him be part of the so-called "rebuild."

I approached Torre about the Montanez deal and reminded him that he'd promised me I'd be playing every day. He seemed lukewarm when I brought it up, almost noncommittal. And by the time the season went from April into May, I had become nothing more than a pinch-hitter, with a spot start here and there. Montanez was playing every day at first, and I wasn't given a chance to break into the outfield. I didn't even start a game in July, and went more than two months in between starts. We fell out of it early and by mid-August dropped into last place for good.

My mother was a very strict disciplinarian, and she taught me that your word or a handshake meant something. She was my inspirational leader at home and she had to be my mother and my father at the same time, so she kept a close watch on me. All I ever expected was being treated fairly and honestly, and to this day it is why I give everybody equal time and I treat everybody with respect and a handshake is a deal.

Torre and I shook hands when he told me he'd play me every day, but he didn't keep his word on it. I didn't know what happened after he became the manager. I guess he thought he was smarter than everybody and knew everything. But he pushed aside a few people like me and never gave me an opportunity. He let you rot. A good manager utilizes his players or gets rid of them. If you don't have use for a guy, trade him. Just letting me sit there rotting away was a waste of time for everybody. Sitting on a bench the entire season with fewer than 100 at-bats was ridiculous. And for somebody pinch hitting as well as I did, you would have thought they could have played me more.

I don't know whether he was jealous of the relationship I had with Joan Payson, Donald Grant, or the fans. I had been there for so long, and then he just put me on the side to dry out after making a promise. He let me deteriorate right in front of everybody, and there was nothing I could do about it. He made his moves, and he showed his colors, and I didn't get along with him after that. That was surprising because I did room with him, and we were close before he became manager. We talked baseball all the time, so he had to know I knew what I was talking about.

I had just one year left on a three-year contract, so playing as little as I did wasn't gonna generate any great offers when I became a free agent. And I wasn't interested in going anywhere else. As I looked around the clubhouse, I had become the elder statesman and remembered being a young kid joining the club and getting advice from guys like Gil Hodges and Duke Snider. And as the players' representative, the young guys were coming to me with any questions or concerns, asking for advice all the time. I'd always tried to defend them when I could and enjoyed that part of it. If somebody had a problem, we'd take a vote on it as a democracy. And I'd watch trade after trade, and guys getting released that sent my friends to other teams, guys I'd developed relationships with.

Our ballclub fell apart after '69. Johnny Murphy died, and that's when it all went downhill with Joe McDonald and his guys, who were totally incompetent. They got taken all the time on trades. Lorinda de Roulet took over the ballclub and she certainly wasn't accustomed to running a baseball club. She listened to McDonald and took his side on everything. And then they pushed aside Grant and had no control of things after that. Once Torre came into the front office, I made a couple comments that the Mets had termites, and what I meant by that was their internal structure was very weak. Elevating McDonald to general manager ruined the whole organization. Then we lost Whitey Herzog, who would have been a great manager. It crumbled right then. It went downhill in a hurry.

But the funny thing is that I wanted to stay. There was so much drama surrounding the team and so much negativity. It should have been easy for me to say I wanted to leave. The fun was mostly gone by now, and I was sick of the losing and not playing. It was no different now than in the early years, but I thought I could be part of the solution and not part of the problem. I was helping the young guys and liked that part, so even in my reduced role I felt I was making a difference. I was getting closer to retirement but thought I was good for three or four more years, whatever. I had a year ahead of me to think about signing a new contract or test the free-agency market. But I knew to get either one, I'd need to play on a more regular basis.

You had time to think about such things over the winter. It was easy to vacillate because you knew the improvements made to club in the off-season weren't gonna be enough, that the New York Yankees and other big spenders were grabbing up all the superstars to improve their clubs. It was hard to imagine that we'd fallen so far so fast, and even being part of the New York market, the club couldn't afford to go after guys like Reggie Jackson, Tommy John, Don Gullett, and Goose Gossage who all signed on the other side of town with the Yankees. It was disheartening.

Little by little, the Mets club from '69 had been dismantled. The only guys remaining were me and Koosman. Sure, it had been almost 10 years, but it seemed like a New York minute to me. There'd been some rumors of Koosman getting dealt a few times, but when it happened in December of '78, I was the last man in the room standing.

They traded Koosman to the Minnesota Twins, and we got Jesse Orosco in return. Orosco ended up having a darn good career, as it turns out. He didn't come in with a lot of flash. He was very consistent over a long time. He had a rubber arm and could pitch forever. But still, Koosman was a star in New York like Seaver was. Koosman had some down years with us lately, but for many of us back in the day, we felt he was the stopper on the club, and Seaver was the franchise player who got most of the publicity. Of course, Seaver deserved all he got, and we always felt confident playing behind him. But there was something about Koosman's makeup that was a little different than Seaver's. Other than Sandy Koufax, I thought Koosman was the best lefty pitcher in the league. True, he'd come off two bad years in a row, but we didn't give him much run support. The fact that he was in his mid-30s and the Mets were on a rebuilding phase made some sense, and for once the Mets were dealing instead of acquiring an older pitcher. But it was hard to see him go. And as was our history, Koosman roared back and won 20 that year. Happened to us all the time.

By the time the '79 season rolled around, about the only good things that happened to me were appearing on the cover of *Sports Illustrated*, causally eating a lobster on a table. By that time, I'd become known as the best pinch-hitter in baseball, so it was all a parody that I could relax and enjoy the game because I wouldn't be making an appearance until later on. Then, in spring training, I made an appearance on *Saturday Night Live*.

The show was such a huge hit back then that people were staying home on Saturday nights or at least coming home early to watch the show. They brought the crew down to our spring training facilities in St. Petersburg and filmed a skit that had a fictional baseball player named Chico Escuela, a retired, former All-Star ballplayer (Garrett Morris) trying out for the club. The Chico character had already become quite popular on the show, so anybody who watched *SNL* knew who he was.

As part of the skit, Bill Murray talked about a tell-all book Chico had written (*Bad Stuff 'Bout The Mets*) and was trying to stir things up, asking questions from the book to some of the real Mets. He asked a few questions to Nelson Briles and Steve Henderson, then came over to me and wanted to know what I thought about Chico accusing me of stealing his soap and never giving it back to him. I was at first base taking throws from the infielders, sort of ignoring the question, but when Murray wanted to know if it was true that Seaver used to take up two parking spaces, I just said that wasn't true. When the show came out a few weeks later, it was hilarious and quite popular. We all wanted to be part of it, so I guess I was one of the lucky ones.

But the old saying that truth is stranger than fiction could have been what '79 was to me. I'd been through enough of these scenarios with new guys coming in to know better. I could see I wasn't gonna play much again and had nothing to lose at this point, so on one occasion when I did say something to Torre, he said he just wanted me around. But around for what? But I figured it out that he was picking my brain on the bench during the games. But I wanted more playing time, not to be another coach.

He did play me in right for about a week in May, probably filling in for some injured player. But it was back to pinch hitting after that. Meanwhile, Montanez was struggling all year to stay above .200 with hardly any home runs or RBIs, and so they traded him in August to the Texas Rangers. Again, it was just so typical of the Mets to give up on a guy having a bad year, but

looking at the current roster, I knew I'd get more of a chance
to play against righties. And there we were in last place again,
20 games out, playing in front of small crowds, and headed for
100 losses, which we avoided by one loss. During the three-year
contract I signed, we'd finished last each year with over 90
losses in each season. The old Mets weren't only on my mind,
but the press was all over those comparisons. In the off-season,
I took a look at all that and knew I'd come about as full circle
as a player can.

I wasn't interested in going out of New York, so I really
didn't pursue free agency. Dick Moss was my agent and he knew
what my feelings were. The thought of just moving from New
York to participate with another team really didn't excite me.
But I wanted to keep playing. I was only 34 and was gonna be
35 that winter. Basically, I was set for life but wasn't interested
in packing up and leaving New York, and baseball wasn't much
fun anymore when you're on a bad ballclub. And I never spoke
to the Yankees. They signed Bob Watson as a free agent to play
first base, but aside from that, I didn't even know what George
Steinbrenner was doing and didn't pay attention to what he
was doing.

But my attention had turned to the bigger picture. At some
point in '79, I found out from the Payson family that the club
was gonna be for sale. So I was one of the first ones to jump
on that and took the opportunity in August to put a group
together with intentions of going into the front office. I wasn't
playing anyway, so I put together a group and was approached
by Bob Abplanalp, a very influential man whose company made
precision valves. He asked if I had a group of investors, then
he offered me to join him and said our group would run out
of funds and he was right. We needed more than we thought,

so after figuring out what he had to say was right, I knew I'd probably be better off going with him.

My thought at that point was that it would be great to start a career, which I thought I was gonna have in the front office. I was thinking about it and knew I never wanted to be a manager, because I didn't have the temperament to be dealing with players one-on-one and listening to all the excuses on why they can't perform. It wasn't for me. I always wanted to go to the front office working above the manager, making all the deals and transitions and not have to deal with the player. I wanted to handle the internal stuff, and that was my goal. Grant knew that was what I wanted to do, and I think it would have happened if he had more authority at the end. I think he was being pushed aside by de Roulet, and McDonald had more control of the ballclub, which hurt me big time in the end.

So I joined his group, and he got me involved by first asking that I set up a meeting between himself and de Roulet. I got them together in August, and we tried to negotiate, but de Roulet began her stalling tactics right from the start. She wanted to sell the ballclub, but she kept hedging after that initial meeting. She wanted to sell, she didn't want to sell, but she kept postponing her decision and kept putting him off. At first, she said we'd do it right after the season, then it became at Christmas time, and then after New Year's. It really wasn't a very easy or amicable transition, and Abplanalp wasn't the kind of guy who waited around for a decision to be made. He was in more of a hurry to buy the club and had every intention of having me involved with it, but she didn't give any firm numbers for him to think about. And he just wanted to get it going. He just wanted a number, just a yes or no. It was one of those deals. But she didn't give him any firm numbers for him to think about. She was a very tough businesswoman, but I could tell he was becoming frustrated by her delays.

So it became a mishmash as she kept putting him off. And when Nelson Doubleday and John Pickett came along, Abplanalp wasn't interested in getting into a bidding war and didn't even attend the last meeting with her. All along, de Roulet didn't want to negotiate with him and would rather negotiate with her friends, Doubleday, Pickett, and, to a smaller extent, Fred Wilpon.

As all this was happening, I wasn't sure about where any of it was going to go, so I still kept my door open to being a player/coach on Torre's staff. Torre was the only manager I was friendly with, and I told him several times I wanted to be a player/coach and be his right-hand man and needed his help. I knew I couldn't sign with the Mets with McDonald as GM, and we hadn't spoken a word to each other for three years since my final contract that Grant took care of. I couldn't expect to negotiate a player/coach contract with McDonald. He was holding a grudge against me and it wasn't even worth approaching him. So I asked Torre to intercede for me and I said I wanted to be a player/coach who could mostly pinch hit because that's all he was doing with me anyway. It all came back to him going back on his promise to play me every day, so I thought he owed me. I got my bunions taken care of when they asked, and that was a nasty surgery.

When he said he couldn't help me, I was on my own. I couldn't believe he was being so standoffish. We'd been friends all these years, and he confided in me with things affecting the club. I was really his off-the-field assistant, but he insisted he couldn't help me. When he said all that to me, I knew he was just looking out for himself and wouldn't help me, so I thought to myself, *What kind of friend is this?* So I really had words with him at the end and didn't want to be his friend anymore. I didn't talk to him the last two weeks of the season, and once the season ended, he went one way, and I went the other way. And to this day, I want nothing to do with him. He had no backbone. I really didn't want to do anything after that because Torre really soured me on baseball. I didn't even want to help in the minor league systems, and nobody was calling me anyway. We were so close, and he didn't help me in the end. Is that what you do for your friends?

I was surprised with the way Torre handled things when he first took over as manager because I thought he was capable of setting the tone like Hodges did in '68. Instead, he came in for the ride and became a yes man. He was probably pretty smart in doing so because he ended up with a long career in baseball as a manager and then working for Major League Baseball. He bullshitted everybody, and it seemed as if his past got him a lot of positions in baseball. But people who know him, know the real person of what he turned out to be. He turned out to be a real phony. I thought he was my friend, and it turns out he was probably my biggest enemy. Torre got to where he is today by stepping over and on lots of people.

With McDonald and Torre running the club, it was easy to keep me on the outs. I had no one to go to by then. They ran the organization down and eventually were forced to sell the ballclub because of what they did to it internally. The Mets had termites. They had incompetent people and they killed it. Herzog left the club. He had a disagreement and didn't get promoted and wound up leaving the Mets and became a great manager. He was good at evaluating young talent. So the good people in the organization were gone, and all the friends and the negative people stayed on. McDonald became the right-hand man to de Roulet. And what did she know about baseball? She was born into a wealthy family and she was running the club with McDonald, and I knew it wouldn't go anywhere. Anybody who knew anything about baseball knew that.

Looking around baseball at that time, guys who got fired from one organization were hired by another. They'd get the same job. If you're bad in one organization, you were gonna be bad in another organization. It was the same losers going from one organization to another, and then suddenly they looked smart when they happen to manage better teams that had nothing to do with them. But that's what baseball used to do. It was the good-boy network. It's not right when new people don't get an opportunity, and I'm not saying this just about myself. I'm saying this about many others who were in the same boat I was in. People like me who should have stayed in the game but never got an opportunity. I knew everybody back in the '70s. I knew their strengths and weaknesses. I followed the game. I had the love of baseball and thought I could help. When that didn't happen, it rocked my world...a complete disappointment not to have an opportunity with the new ownership.

It was just bad timing, and my timing stunk as far as that's concerned. Look at the relationships I had with the important people in the organization. Hodges died. Grant got pushed aside. Mrs. Payson died. Those were people who liked me and respected me. I think I would have had an opportunity to have been in the front office had any one of those three things not happened. But things happened, and I got pushed aside.

I went from the penthouse to the outhouse of opportunity. Wanting to still be a player or coach or transitioning to the front office, I thought something very special was going to happen. Then the bottom fell out. I was probably sort of in a depression because my life turned at that point with no more opportunities in the organization I played my whole life for. And then new ownership came in and brought in an outsider like Frank Cashen, who had a Baltimore mentality. I don't think he had any great feelings for anybody that was with the Mets during that transition, so he wasn't bringing in anybody to work around him, especially since he didn't know us, he didn't know me. He might have figured I could stab him in the back or something like that, so I never had any relationship with him. Not to say he wasn't a good person or baseball mind. He was Baltimore, I was the Mets, and so I was on the outside. He brought me around and he could have been thinking, *This guy is looking to take my job.*

I think all of that played on my mind some in a game we played against the Houston Astros late in the season. I wasn't much anymore for sticking around the clubhouse after a game, so when Jeff Leonard made what I thought was the final out of the game, I bolted from first base to the locker room.

But someone had called timeout before the final pitch, so without me at first base, Leonard came back to the plate and hit a single. I still didn't know what was going on or why I was the only guy in the locker room. So somebody came back in and told me what had happened, so I rushed back out to my position. I didn't do it intentionally, but how could the umpires not realize the first baseman was missing? The whole thing became a big deal after that with the managers playing a protest game with each other. That really was a dichotomy of another lost season.

It was close to spring training when I decided I didn't want to be involved with the club anymore. We were a last-place team, I wasn't starting, and then this fiasco. I was so disgusted with baseball, I just said I was done. I never even sent in my retirement papers and never told anyone, I just didn't show up at spring training. McDonald wasn't gonna bring me to spring training, and Torre wasn't gonna help me. Everything that could go wrong did go wrong. I could see the writing on the wall. They were going in a different direction. And that's when I decided it was over for me. It probably was my mistake. It was immaturity on my part, and I should have pursued something else with baseball. But I was so disgusted, I didn't even try. Then they lost another 95 games in 1980. They had nothing after the season, just disarray.

That's my biggest disappointment, that I didn't stay in baseball. I never had an offer from the Mets organization to coach or do anything for them. I ended up leaving on bad terms. I lost contact with the Mets once I wasn't involved and was soon out of the loop and wasn't paying attention to baseball anymore. Once I got out, I went right to work doing my own thing and really wasn't following baseball. I used to follow the game and knew the stats of all the players, but once I retired, I lost touch. I've always been loyal to the Mets organization and never wanted to go outside of it. I was a New Yorker, and they gave me my chance. They made a good pick of me in the draft and got 18 years of service out of me. And with the way the Mets wheeled and dealed, that's saying something.

I had several conversations with Wilpon a number of years later when I got friendly with him again. One day at the Brooklyn Cyclones game when I was doing some TV work, he was there and he called me to his box, and I told him he had just hired the wrong guy. I told him that non-New Yorkers couldn't handle the press like a native New Yorker could, and I told him I'd manage the club and get him more wins, and if I didn't, he wouldn't have to pay me.

Nothing came of that. He told me I had to go to the minor leagues first to learn how to manage, and I told him I didn't believe in that concept. You know the game, or you don't know the game. You have to deal with the press and you have to deal with people. He thought I was trying to come in without going to the minor leagues, but I thought I had the capabilities of doing that. I thought the toughest thing about managing in New York was the press, and by surrounding yourself with the best baseball people around, you let them do the work and you take care of the press by being as honest and straightforward as can be.

And that's why I got along with the press. When the press came to my locker, they knew they were gonna get an honest answer. I wasn't gonna go and hide out in the next room trying to avoid them. Why? Because I missed a ground ball or made an error? No. I gave them the truth. If it hit a pebble, and they knew it hit a pebble, I would tell them that and I never made excuses. I was always there. Some of the guys would go into the clubhouse and hide out and they'd write the story anyway, so you might as well tell them. If I told a writer what happened that I missed a ground ball that went through my legs and felt like shit about it, what are they gonna write? If they asked me why I struck out in a certain spot, I'd say I was looking for a curveball, and he threw me a fastball. So they got their answer and they knew the answer because some of them knew the game, and you couldn't bullshit them. That's the type of front-office guy or bench coach I would have been. It's too bad I never got my chance.

Chapter 17

HEALTH, WEALTH, AND HOLLYWOOD

THE LAST YEAR I played was when I started noticing when I was sitting on the bench that I was having trouble seeing the outfield scoreboard and signs. During the year, it was getting fuzzy at times, and other times it was clear as day. But I didn't take any action right away. Then right after the season, I was watching the playoffs on TV, and the screen would be fuzzy sometimes. I was losing weight, and I thought that was a good thing and was happy about that, but I wasn't trying to lose weight. So I lost five pounds, then 10 pounds, then 15 pounds. When I lost 20 pounds, I figured I should go get it checked out by the doctor. That's when they told me my sugar levels were out of whack, and the levels were at 600, which is very, very high, and they told me I had diabetes. They put me on insulin right away.

It was so high they wanted to put me in the hospital, but I talked them out of it, so they said I had to start injecting myself. They gave me a syringe and told me to practice on myself and I said, "Practice on myself?" I had never given myself a needle and I wasn't looking to practice poking myself with an inch long needle, so I said, "Can I practice on an orange?" And he said to do whatever I wanted to do, but I had to practice.

As soon as I started taking insulin, the weight loss stopped, and I didn't have to go to the hospital. Then I got it down far enough where I could take pills instead of the injections. I started taking a few drugs, and when the companies found out who I was, they hired me as a spokesman to do some public relations that included speaking engagements around the country. Eventually, a law went into effect that prohibited the pharmaceutical companies from promoting their drugs with spokesman like myself, ending that job for me and many others.

I stayed to myself for a few years after the diabetes diagnosis and didn't feel well for a couple of years until I learned how to control that disease. I just stayed away from the game, and once you stay away, you kind of alienate yourself from baseball. If you don't go mingling around and keep friends, you lose that camaraderie you had in baseball. I did lose touch and still had no thoughts about doing anything after that or getting back into the game. My good friends in baseball were still my three old roommates, Tug McGraw, Ron Swoboda, Jon Matlack, and, of course, Cleon Jones. Once the game was ended and our careers were over, they all went home just like I did. But we stayed in touch. I didn't go to the ballpark much either. On occasion, I would go to a game and I always stayed loyal as a New York Mets fan because it was the only organization that I knew.

I may have retired from baseball but still needed to work. I was only 35 years of age, and a baseball pension wasn't nearly enough to survive on. The fact that free agency started at around the same time I was about to retire was more of that timing thing that for some reason rarely worked out in my favor. But I was grateful for what Marvin Miller did for us. Miller did a great job of negotiating with guarantees and such.

For one thing, the minimum salaries went up after he took charge. It's hard to believe, looking back now, how low our salaries were.

Back in the early years, you always got a job during the winter to try to supplement your salary. Your salary ended on the last day of the season and you had nothing to live off of unless you put some money away. Making $6,000 or $7,000 or $10,000, that wasn't enough for most of us to take the winter off and not work. I became a stockbroker and got my license when I turned 21 and I made good money with a good firm.

And in the early years, we never had agents to help negotiate our salaries. They didn't exist back then. When you started in Major League Baseball back then, you signed your own contract like I did with the Mets, and that was a large bonus at that time. But once you were in the game, they frowned upon agents. They were smart. They knew if they negotiated with the player one on one, that would make it pretty difficult to representative yourself and speak to a guy like George Weiss, who's been in the game for a long time and was a tough negotiator. Once they started talking about all your negatives, they never really talked about the positives. And when they brow beat you long enough, you're looking to pay them to sign a contract!

And there was nothing really for them to negotiate in the first year or two when you're making the minimum. I think we all made the same, around $6,000, then it went up to $7,000. There's nothing to negotiate because everyone started with that. Even the guys who became stars all had low starting salaries. Every year after the season, you had to go in and negotiate again, and when you have a bad ballclub that loses 100 games, you don't have a lot of good things to talk about. So when Weiss starts on you, it's a lot of negative statistics unless you had a great year, then it's pretty tough for them to say you can't hit. Even Mickey Mantle had trouble signing because he negotiated for himself. They took your numbers, and numbers don't lie. It's the same way in business. You don't have much to say for yourself when you finish last and you hit .240.

It was tough negotiating because the longer you sat in that office, the more depressed you got because they'd start talking about how you can't throw or you can't run. It's pretty easy for them to pick and choose over all the negative statistics. And they had the numbers in front of him; we didn't. I made the All-Star team when I was 20, but I didn't come out with a 10-year contract. I came out with a one-year contract. It took me a while in my career, but thanks to Miller, I signed a three-year, multi-year contract at the end. A nice contract but not enough to sit back and enjoy the scenery.

So I got involved in a display manufacturing company right after retirement. I used to manufacture displays for companies, and my hobby was woodwork, so I found companies that needed racks to hold their products. I designed and manufactured displays. I stayed, but did I love it? No. Sometimes you end up taking jobs you really don't want to, but you have to. You're out of baseball, you're out of work, and you still need to make a living. But I didn't like the commute from near Giants Stadium to Long Island, so I finally parted ways.

I can't say I kept a close eye on the Mets, but I paid attention to what was going on. I had such a sour taste in my mouth, I didn't want to be around baseball anymore, didn't want any parts of it. But I knew they had another 95-loss season in '80, and that came as no surprise to me. I knew what was going on in baseball with the players' strike in '81 and how the Mets were doing when the strike came in June. Another horrible record, that's what. And with my old pals Rusty Staub and Dave Kingman back in New York sharing first-base duties, I could only have imagined how much playing time I would have had. When the Mets parted ways with Joe Torre at the end of the year and proved he couldn't manage, I wondered what took them so long.

Just when I thought that baseball had completely forgotten about me, Swoboda and I were contacted by some Hollywood producer to get involved in the filming of a new baseball movie they were shooting in Buffalo called *The Natural* with Robert Redford as the star. They wanted us to give batting and fielding tips to a bunch of non-baseball playing actors to help them look the part of a professional player. We didn't do it, but after the whole thing was over and we saw the movie, I had my regrets.

But I didn't know that much about it. All I knew was that we'd have to spend six weeks in Buffalo at scale pay, and that didn't appeal to me. I'd lived in Buffalo before when I was in the minors and I wasn't particularly fond of the town. I wasn't looking forward to spending six weeks or more in a place I wasn't fond of.

We were invited to the movie premiere in New York, and turns out it was a great movie. It reminded me at times of my favorite baseball movie going up, *The Pride of the Yankees*. I lived and breathed baseball as a kid, so I loved all those old baseball movies. There was a certain point in the movie when I really regretted not getting involved, and when the movie was over, we went up to Redford and told him he looked like a major league player. In a lot of these movies, most of these guys didn't look at all like baseball players, but Redford had a pretty good swing in that movie. Some of the guys who were helping him and stayed around for the six weeks really improved his ability to play. My old batting practice pitcher, Tony Ferrara, was one of those guys. He ended up in the cast as the technical advisor and the third-base coach.

My wife was disappointed that I didn't sign up for the movie and she said afterward, "How stupid are you?" I reminded her of being in Buffalo for six weeks, but that didn't change her opinion on the decision I'd made. She wasn't happy. But a couple of years later, the new owner of the Buffalo team, Robert Rich, builds this new stadium in Buffalo, thinking eventually they'll get Major League Baseball. He knew baseball was going to expand again, and Buffalo had the demographics that the leagues were looking for. So he invited anybody who played for Buffalo, who had a career in the major leagues to participate in the opening of the stadium. They sent their plane down for me and my wife in New York to pick us up and they flew us to Buffalo for the weekend ceremonies. They put us up in a suite in a nice hotel. We had dinner and went to the ballpark. So we did end up in Buffalo again, just not for six weeks.

I'd always known that playing baseball in New York was hard, but I also knew it had its advantages beyond playing. And I knew another chance to be in another baseball movie like *The Natural* was slim to none. But many years later, appearing on the hit comedy show, *Everybody Loves Raymond*, was close enough for me.

I should have learned my lesson from saying no to *The Natural*, but I was reluctant at first and I did say no. I didn't want to fly out to California. Who knew how long we'd have to be there? I guess the old memories from being in Japan for six weeks may have had something to do with it, but Art Shamsky finally talked some sense into me and said that I had to go, that it's gonna be fun. Because we were close friends, I let him talk me into it and so I went.

It all came together because Brad Garrett, the actor who played Ray Romano's brother, had a dog named Shamsky, and I guess because of that, someone from the show contacted Art Shamsky about it. All the actors on the show were big Mets fans and fans of that '69 club, so they asked a bunch of us from that team, including me, Shamsky, McGraw, Swoboda, Buddy Harrelson, Jerry Grote, and Jones. It ended up taking three days to tape a show that should have taken no time at all. Our parts were very short. I didn't even have any lines at all, and Shamsky had a few words. Two or three guys had some lines, and the episode (*Big Shots*) is still played to this day.

There were so many award winners from that show for years. And those old episodes still run late at night across the country. I still get residual checks to this day. It's not a lot of money, and there were times when I got a couple of pennies in a check. It was crazy to open up the mail and see a check for two cents. I think I got one check that was a penny! It cost them more to print the check and process the Goddamn thing. I should have kept it instead of cashing it. The reason why some checks were so low were because of what the Screen Actors Guild took out for dues. The check might have started out at $150, but by the time they took out all your dues, you might be lucky getting a dollar. It was worse than having taxes taken out from your regular paycheck.

But my favorite types of shows have always been the westerns. When I was a kid, I watched a lot of westerns. *Rawhide* with Clint Eastwood, Bonanza, shows like that. I liked the cowboys and Indians movies and shows, and there were a lot of them in the time I grew up. John Wayne, Roy Rogers, all these guys. I still watch them whenever one comes on at nighttime. Whenever there was a new western type movie coming out when we were on the road, that's what we loved to do during our free time. I just liked watching the action and not sitting there trying to figure out the plot.

Now I like *Shark Tank* and *Jeopardy!* shows. I've seen all the *Shark Tank* shows and follow the businesses the sharks went after. I love the way the sharks position themselves and watching guys like Mark Cuban usually outbid all the others to take advantage of the best deals. He's sharp. He knows all the electronic businesses and, secondly, he waits until the end when he offers more money than the other sharks, and they usually jump on it. Money talks. I like *Jeopardy!* and am always amazed at the level of knowledge people have and the ability to answer so quickly. I guess I like both shows because it sort of reminds me of playing baseball and how competitive it is, how only the best competitors get to go on even after working hard to make it on the show. There's always been a fine line between winning and losing or making it or getting cut. Those shows remind me of what I went through and what others before and after me went through and how so many guys who never made it to the big leagues kept trying. There's a great spirit and resolve shown by the people in these shows, and thinking about it now, I consider myself that kind of person by what I've been through and seen.

There are only a few times during a career while the season is in progress when you get a chance to think about people who have made their mark or are on their way to making one. The season just moves too fast. But when you're as young as I was in the beginning, you have a different focus and mind-set.

I was 18 when the Mets played an exhibition game at West Point against the U.S. military team. I was younger than some of those cadets and gave no thought at the time about what these boys may have had in store for them. Being that my dad had been killed in the second World War, I was exempt from the draft or ever having to serve. And I had friends who went off to Vietnam, and some of them never came back. I wasn't oblivious to all that, never took any of it for granted, but never really thought about it either. I was one of the lucky ones and all I cared about was playing well and winning the game.

There were certain things I didn't know at the time that I know now. Things that help you appreciate the world from another perspective. Our pitching coach was Ernie White, a guy I had very little interactions with. All of us were aware of the number of big-name guys who'd served in war, giving up prime playing years to serve their country. Bob Feller, Ted Williams, and Warren Spahn to name a few. And White was another one of those special guys. I wondered how many more Ernie Whites there were out there.

White had a nice career as a pitcher in the major leagues. He played on pennant winning clubs, and beat the New York Yankees once in a World Series game. I never took the time to know any of this back then. I knew the stars and what they did in their careers, but I wasn't especially tuned into the war years and the time they all missed. And I wasn't tuned into the careers of guys like White who not only went to war, but participated in the Battle of The Bulge. No doubt he was one of those heroes who flew under the radar.

We went to Cooperstown to play the Washington Senators in the annual Hall of Fame game. We lost that game, but that was secondary for most of us. I'd never been to Cooperstown before and was anxious to visit the Hall of Fame. I respected Cooperstown and looked up to all the guys enshrined here.

I took some time going down row after row inside the Hall, reading the plaques of all the greats of the game, and I visualized that one day somebody would be reading my plaque. That's the one place you want to go. I thought about it as a kid and then when I got signed. I listened to all the hype, I read all the stories and predictions, and with a little luck along the way, I hoped one day I'd get in there. We went back to Cooperstown for another exhibition game 12 years later, and in those 12 years I'd grown from the wide-eyed boy I was to a man face to face with his past.

I went back into the Hall of Fame and read many of the same plaques I had 12 years earlier. I took more time to explore where they had uniforms, gloves, and spikes worn by the greats. Babe Ruth, Lou Gehrig, Honus Wagner, and I appreciated all of it so much more. I thought about Gil Hodges—another war veteran who gave up a few years of baseball—and why he wasn't enshrined. And I thought about star players like Hodges who weren't in. As I thought about all that, I knew right then that Ed Kranepool would never have a plaque at the Hall of Fame.

I wasn't devastated by that reality. It was sort of a mixed feeling. I might have been a bit disappointed in myself and thought maybe I'd let some people down who's always pegged me for the HOF, but I looked at those guys who weren't in...and it hit me how difficult it was to make it as a Hall of Famer. Before you knew it, we were whisked away and back on the road for another game in another city, leaving my thoughts behind. But they stayed with me in the back of my mind.

I look at all this today in a far different way than I did back then. Maturity has its advantages. Young guys in the military giving their lives for their countries. The old baseball players—great or good or even average players—sacrificing career for the country. My father. My friends. All of them paved the way for me. It would have been nice if my plaque was hanging in Cooperstown. But maybe it wasn't such a big deal after all.

Chapter 18

A MIRACLE OR TWO

MY DIABETES WAS PROBABLY HEREDITARY. My mother had it late in life and wound up passing away from it. Type 2 has nothing to do with diet; it's just hereditary. I had all kinds of trouble with my feet and eventually I had surgery on my toes about 10 years ago that was caused by the diabetes and the poor circulation I had. They cut off one toe at first, hoping to salvage the other four, but that didn't work, and they wound up taking a couple more and finally they cut the side of my foot, and I lost all my toes and the big bone on the side of my foot. I had three surgeries in all on my left foot. They made a special shoe for me that allows me to walk about 60% of my normal walk. But I don't have the balance when I stand straight, and that's why I try to stay close to a wall to get my balance for a little support.

My wife and I used to go out to dinner a lot, and we'd run into her friends all the time in the restaurants. On the way out, she would stop and talk to them and I would say hello fast and keep walking. She kept saying to me that I was rude, very rude, because I didn't stay around and talk. That's when I explained to her I had no balance, and if I stayed any longer, I was gonna fall in their soup. That would be embarrassing in the middle of the dining room. After that, she understood. Now she's conscious of that and makes sure I have a place to lean on or hold something so I can balance myself. I can still drive and I'm fortunate it was my left foot.

It's difficult to walk any great distance because you have to compensate and it's easy to lose your balance. That's why I'm using my cane more and more. If I walk, it's not too bad, but if I stop, that's when I run into a problem. Art Shamsky's girlfriend made my New York Mets cane for me. She's in that business and created canes with team logos for all the MLB teams.

Diabetes creates a lot of problems. About two years after my surgery, I thought I was having a heart attack, and then my lungs filled up with water. They rushed me to the hospital and they took some tests and ran my blood work, and that's when I was told I didn't have a heart attack, but that I had a problem with my kidneys. I ended up getting kidney failure. And after a couple of years of taking drugs, they came to me and recommended dialysis or a kidney transplant. Getting a transplant was easier said than done. I'd learned that over 100,000 Americans were on a wait list for a kidney, and for each one who was on that list, the wait could be five years or more. And being that I was over 70, the risks were high for a problem during or after surgery. I thought about my options, and it got so bad that dialysis had become a very real thing.

But I'd need to go three times a week, and yes, it would be a life-changer and a lifesaver at the same time. My whole life would change on the spot. I couldn't go anywhere. I would've been sort of in a box. Alive, but not living. I was smart enough to know what was going on with the dialysis option of changing your life to no quality of life. I would've been really stuck to my own house, sort of like a house arrest, but different. I'd read that after receiving a dialysis treatment, you feel like shit right after it, then tomorrow you're feeling better, then the next day the cycle starts again. It may sound selfish, but I loved to travel, and going on cruises was my favorite activity. I'd been on 35 cruises, and COVID changed all that. And now this. I wasn't feeling sorry for myself and was trying not to let it get me down, but you can't take a cruise or even go away for a few days on dialysis. I really needed to find a donor.

There are three types of people in this world: people that watch things happen, people that don't know what's happening, and people that make things happen. You don't have to figure out what category you're in. I needed a kidney, so I couldn't make it happen. And being a Met all my life helped me get the publicity needed to spread the word. My tenure in New York and the relationship I had with the writers really helped me. I never gave them any reasons to hold a grudge against me. There was no stress approaching them. I didn't burn any bridges like I may have with Joe McDonald. And this was no game. This was life and death.

They said they would put me on the donor list, and I had to choose a hospital. I looked at Hackensack and Stony Brook and decided on Stony Brook. They were wonderful. We did a lot of promotion searching, beginning with family or friends and anyone we knew. We knew a lot of people, and they knew me. Plenty of people wanted to donate and came forward hoping for a match.

The writers started coming around and wrote their articles. Then the radio stations and the TV stations joined in. It was right around that same time when my relationship with the Mets started to heal. The way it all ended for me in 1980 never sat well with me. It made me bitter thinking about it sometimes, that I'd given 18 years and just like that was an afterthought. I looked around at the other teams, and they'd treated their veterans with respect. As guys retired after I did, I watched them get coaching jobs, announcing jobs, analyst jobs. Some became managers. Others went into the front office. Some had their numbers retired or a special day for them at a home game. I was a meet-and-greet guy, shaking hands occasionally with people in the luxury boxes. I was more than a greeter and knew I belonged in the front office, doing a better job than they had. And as I watched all this from afar, it started to bother me.

I think that all came to a head when I had an argument with Jeff Wilpon during a team banquet in 2012 or 2013. There was still some bad blood with the way the Mets deal went down in 1980. We both said some things. I felt justified in what I had to say, but I knew when it was all over, I'd taken a step backward with the organization, sort of like I did when I talked back to Gil Hodges years ago. I didn't know if I'd ever get back in the good graces of the Mets. I don't know if my health issues had anything to do with it, but Wilpon extended the olive branch to me in 2018. To have Wilpon call and invite me and my wife back in was special for us. I apologized to him for anything I may have said that may have offended him. It's hard holding onto bitterness and resentment for so long, and when we talked, a great weight had been lifted off my shoulders.

I threw out the ceremonial first pitch at a Mets home game in August and for the first time in years felt part of it again. On top of my foot surgery, I'd had rotator cuff surgery a few years earlier and could barely lift my arm to make even the one throw. I may not have thrown a strike, but I didn't care. I looked around this beautiful stadium and thought back to when we vacated the Polo Grounds for Shea Stadium and found some irony in all that. Time stays still for no one. And like people, stadiums come and go. They crumble and fall apart with age, just like people. Just like me.

But all this gave us the much-needed publicity to find a donor. But there were no matches, and after a while, we started running out of people coming forward. Then the Wilpons brought in Jay Horwitz to help me promote it. Horwitz was always one of those guys who made a difference, and I knew he would now. He did everything possible, setting up websites, emails, and phone numbers for people to contact him. He kept a file at his office at the ballpark. It was through the Mets and their efforts that really helped me there. It was almost to the point where I was gonna go on dialysis. Then the big story came out that they found a kidney donor through Stony Brook.

Turns out the guy was a police officer that volunteered to be my donor, but the story takes an odd twist. After the doctors said it was a good match, they told me it was also a match for a fireman in the hospital who'd been on dialysis and looking for a donor for two to three years. His wife took the tests to see if her kidney was a match, and when the test came back, she was not a match for her husband but was the perfect match for me. The doctor, Frank Darras, asked me to switch, and so I volunteered to take the fireman's wife's kidney, and the fireman took the police officer's. The unbelievable turn of events was now going to save the lives of both us.

Darras proposed that he do the operations at the same time, and so we took his advice. He took the two donors first, then took me and the fireman (Al Barbieri) after they were prepped. When we woke up after surgery, Darras told us the surgeries went off without a hitch. We rested for a few days, then on the fourth day following surgery, they held a press conference, but by then, we'd made national news. The following day, we were able to walk out of the hospital on our own. That became a tremendous story for the kidney foundation, saving two people the same day with two donors by performing four surgeries at the same time. It became a huge story everywhere, the story of the police officer, a fireman, a wife, and an ex-baseball player.

We still stay in touch with each other, but the policeman donor has remained anonymous.

What are the odds of that happening? You take all the people who'd been screened, find the one solitary match, and in the same hospital, they find a pair of matches from that? It's mind-boggling, to say the least. Almost as if a higher power was orchestrating the whole event. Really, how could all that have been by a strange coincidence or luck? They may have called us The Miracle Mets, but that was nothing compared to this. That was my miracle, and little did I know we'd have two miracles after my wife got sick.

A couple of years later, I wanted to move to Florida because the New York weather was always so cold and damp half the years and was really getting to me. One of the side effects of diabetes is the loss of feeling, and the cold weather made it tough to move around, especially with the snow and ice. With bad feet, it was easy to stumble and hard to get up. It was time for a change of scenery, so I figured the quality of life in Florida would be much improved. I discussed it with my wife, and we agreed that we would give it a try, and in the summer, we'd come back to New York. We sold our condo in one week, and I sold off a lot of my sports memorabilia before that. But that was my choice. There were rumors I had to sell some of it off to raise money for the operation, but that wasn't it at all. I knew we'd eventually be moving and didn't want to take all that stuff with us, so we created our own auction. People wanted a lot of that stuff more than I did, so we sold whatever people wanted. Then we left for Florida in October 2021. That's when Monica started feeling sick as soon as we got to Florida. They did some workups on her after she started losing weight and found out she had a mass in her stomach area that turned out to be pancreatic cancer.

You think everything is going to be rosy when making a move like we did. My life was getting back to normal, we're moving into a warmer climate, then everything turned to shit. When you get a diagnosis like that, everything about the world stops right in front of you. That kind of puts a damper on everything. We had rented an apartment in Florida and now we had to start treatments, but we had no idea on how to find the right doctor. It was another challenge we weren't ready for. At least in New York, when I was sick, we knew the turf and had friends and connections everywhere. Over the years I had met many wonderful people, and some happened to be doctors.

One such friend, David Dines, was one of the Mets doctors from my playing days. He suggested a friend at the Cleveland Clinic and a few other places, so I started to search for doctors to get an idea what we were dealing with. Just like the staff at Stony Brook, they were wonderful down at the Cleveland Clinic and certainly did everything they could to help us. They recommended certain treatments, gave us all the what ifs, and when one thing led to another, we had the family all together to discuss the options.

We liked what their theory was but still wanted to explore other options. My wife wanted at least another opinion, and so we checked out Sloan Kettering, then the University of Miami's Sylvester Cancer Center. There was a hospital in Texas, and another one in Tampa, but we had to move fast after months of looking because time is against you when you have pancreatic cancer. I wanted to get down to Sloan Kettering in Florida but didn't have any personal contacts, and that's when someone suggested I contact Fred Wilpon. Wilpon is a very philanthropic man, so I got on the phone and called Wilpon and asked him if he had any contacts at Sloan Kettering and he jumped on it right away. He made a phone call to Sloan and he contacted a buddy who'd been the head of the department at one time and called me back with the guy's number. After that contact I immediately sent them my wife's records. When they looked at her records, they came up with the same way to treat it as the Cleveland Clinic. Next thing you know, out of the blue, we get a phone call from Dr. Nipun Merchant from the University of Miami Sylvester clinic who wanted to meet with us. I called and asked some questions about him, and they all said he was the best man to do this type of surgery.

While we scheduled a meeting with Merchant, the Cleveland Clinic board had met and reversed their original way they planned on proceeding. They were gonna perform chemotherapy first and then the Whipple procedure second, but at the last second, they said they were gonna do surgery first, and then chemo afterward. When I went to see Merchant, he suggested we do the chemo and then the surgery, which was what we all thought was the best approach. He said he didn't have to go through a board to make a decision, that he runs the surgery department. He was adamant about the whole thing. Very decisive. When he sat there and looked me in the eye and told me this was how he was gonna cure my wife, I believed him.

It was the way he spoke with his positive attitude that convinced us he could do it. We jumped on it right away and felt very comfortable with it, and he started in on the chemo process. She was having a little trouble with the chemo and had lost too much weight, so he wanted her to gain back some of the weight back before the surgery. So we gave her every dessert we could think of, and she gained back 20 pounds. When Merchant saw her, he was happy and said, "She's gonna make it. She's going to a beat this thing."

A week later, he said it was time for surgery right now, and we jumped right into it. The surgery lasted six hours. He cut the tumor out, and she went through four more treatments, and he found no signs of cancer. That part was a great ending. I didn't know after that if I was going to get to Cooperstown for Gil Hodges' Hall of Fame induction. I told the Mets if she wasn't feeling well enough, I couldn't leave her in Florida by herself. She went through her fourth treatment just a few days before we came to Cooperstown together for Hodges. I want to give credit to Wilpon and Dr. Dines. I'd had my miracle with my kidney transplant, and now my wife had hers.

Chapter 19

ODD MAN IN

I ALWAYS FOLLOWED THE LEAGUE LEADERS and the standings back when I played, but I was never one to dwell on personal awards or achievements. When it was all said and done and they posted all the categories I topped with the New York Mets, that was pretty humbling. And I'm equally proud of my pinch-hitting records that still stand at No. 1 in the annals of baseball history.

My Mets records are really a testament to how I survived all those years in New York. It takes longevity and some luck to have had all these records. And if you take away that '62 season, I only averaged about 350 plate appearances a year, and that's really just a step above part time. Everything really needs to fall into place to be at the top. I hope the Mets have a player in the future that breaks my records and David Wright's records. But there aren't many guys anymore sticking with one team their whole career, so they may stand for a while.

I knew I never hit a grand slam, and it played on my mind sometimes. All I knew was that there was an opportunity to improve my RBIs statistic and, of course, to help the team win the game. I went to the plate in those situations, just wanting to drive the ball hard somewhere. I used to joke around that I never had one because the bases were never loaded for me. That wasn't quite true. Turns out I had 98 of them.

I may not have hit a single grand slam, but I had 33 hits and knocked in 93 with those 98 at-bats. I had plenty (13) of three-run homers, and two-run homers (39) that amounted to about half of my totals. And I hit 13 home runs off of Hall of Fame pitchers. I did better against some of the better pitchers like Bob Gibson. Maybe I concentrated against those guys. Who knows?

I even found out I'm in the top 10 on the list of guys who hit 100 home runs or more in a career with no grand slams, tied with Bernard Gilkey for 8th place. It's one of those obscure lists I never knew they had until now. There are some pretty big names on that list. The game can be funny with all the statistics there are. Rod Kanehl hit the first ever Mets grand slam in '62. He had a fairly short career, so he couldn't have batted many times (16) with the bases loaded. And look at what Tony Cloninger did in 1966. He hit two in one game and he was a pitcher! And he had nine RBIs in that game! And he didn't have very many (11) home runs in his career. Don Drysdale had one. Other pitchers or part-time guys had one. I guess in my case, it's sort of like a pro golfer playing an entire career without a hole in one. Stuff happens. Go figure.

That's why when you talk about a great clutch hitter or a great RBI guy, it depends on the situations you have. I know there's a ton of new metrics, but back in my day all we had were the totals, and some were misleading and a lot of bullshit to make things look good for a guy. You can't drive in runs if you're on a shit team and there's nobody on base. Had I played on a club like Cincinnati when they had the Big Red Machine, it would have been easy to drive in 100 runs, because every time you come up to bat there'd be Pete Rose or Joe Morgan or one or two other guys on base. Plus, they had speed. One man on or two men on, it's so much easier. And then you get accustomed to being in those situations, and maybe you're not as anxious at the plate with guys on.

You would think being around a long time gave me more chances to win home games (walk-off) in our last at-bat. But I don't recall having that many chances coming up in the bottom of the ninth or in extra innings. We were so far behind in most games with those early Mets teams that there weren't too many opportunities for such things. I did it seven times. I think Rusty Staub and Kevin McReynolds and David Wright eventually passed me, but you gotta give credit to Wilmer Flores for being the leader of that department.

Wes Parker always won the Gold Glove award for first baseman and rightfully so. But never until now did I know where I ranked all time. Turns out I'm in the top 100 in a few categories of defense (No. 67 for fielding percentage with .994 and No. 98 for assists and games played). That's not bad considering how often I was the odd man out.

On the other side of the coin were the no-hitters. The Mets never had a guy hurl a no-hitter during my years. The closest was when Tom Seaver lost his perfect game in the ninth against the Chicago Cubs in '69. But I'd watched or been involved in five, starting with Sandy Koufax's the first day I was a Met. Then we had Jim Bunning throwing a perfect game against us on Father's Day in '64, Bob Moose no-hitting us in '69, followed by Bill Stoneman and Ed Halicki a few years later. We had a few old teammates like Warren Spahn, Don Cardwell, Dean Chance, and Dock Ellis who tossed no-hitters before they were Mets, and, of course, Seaver and Nolan Ryan had theirs after they left us. It was nice to finally see the Mets get that monkey off their backs when Johan Santana tossed a no-hitter in 2012.

I became a proud member of the Mets Hall of Fame in 1990, joining many of my teammates from that '69 club. There are eight guys from that '69 team that are in the Mets Hall of Fame, and that's pretty special to be one of them. I think it's part of the mystique that '69 club brought to the city, that so many guys are honored in this way. Some of the guys, like Seaver and Jerry Koosman, had great careers, and, of course, Seaver is the only one of us that's in the National Baseball Hall of Fame. But the rest of us were good ballplayers in our own right, maybe a little above average as far as statistics go but way above average as teammates and friends.

A lot of times people didn't spend enough time in a Mets uniform to warrant going in. But I think the guys who are in from that era had some kind of cast in the creation of the Mets. From my era of the '60s and '70s and then into the '80s when the Mets became good again, the guys who dominated are in. They've done a good job selecting players for that honor. It's tough putting somebody in who played just one or two years. A lot of times these things are popularity contests based upon who gets nominated, and like the All-Star team, there are oversights.

Except for Tommie Agee, all the other guys (Cleon Jones, Jerry Grote, Buddy Harrelson, Seaver, Koosman, Tug McGraw) were my teammates for about a dozen years or so. With all the moves the Mets made back then, that's really remarkable to have a core of guys that stayed together for so long. There's been about 200 guys traded, released, or sold from the Mets during my career, and the Mets weren't shy about making moves. What you had with this group of guys, you may never see again. I think that's part of the reason why the '69 Mets are still talked about and still relevant. People grew up with us as a team, they experienced the highs and lows of a baseball seasons and of a career. They grew close to guys like Jones,

Harrelson, and all the others, so a part of them left when a guy got traded or retired.

Even our three announcers from back then are in the Mets Hall of Fame. We had the greatest announcers during that time, all with such different personalities. Bob Murphy loved the Mets. He loved the players and never said a negative thing about anybody. Lindsey Nelson was colorful and flamboyant and wore all those wild suits. Ralph Kiner was great because he wanted to talk baseball with you. The other two guys couldn't help us with our hitting, but Kiner was willing to help us with that, and he did that without the authority of the Mets.

It was great being his guest on *Kiner's Korner*. Kiner was a great guy when he interviewed you. He let you talk and say what you wanted and had good baseball comments to make. And you knew if you were on his show, you had a good game. He was a class act and always tried to help the young players. And he had to be careful because the ballclub didn't want him on the field. But he was very positive and snuck in advice when the coast was clear. We didn't have a batting coach all the years I played. They didn't believe in one. They believed in pitching and defense and they had nobody to help you offensively. So Kiner would take you to the side or on the plane or wherever he could find you and he would talk to you if you wanted some help. He was a great player in his day, so he knew what he was talking about. When he tried helping Ron Swoboda when he was striking out all the time, the Mets caught on and they really put it to him, I guess. That was surprising that the Mets frowned upon Kiner giving us advice. That never made any sense to me, or to any of us, for that matter. Here's a guy who's in the Hall of Fame, and instead of taking advantage of his knowledge, they reprimanded him. Go figure.

It was great that Gil Hodges finally got into Cooperstown. The travesty is how long it took for it to happen. You look at his career statistics and you wonder how he was overlooked for so long. I think he was 11th in home runs when he retired, and he won Gold Gloves when they introduced the award in the late '50s. Back in the day and even now, 100 RBIs in a season was the gold standard, and he did it seven straight years and made all those All-Star teams (eight times). And as for grand slams, his totals (14) were off the charts.

I may not have been inducted into Cooperstown, but while I was there supporting Hodges, I couldn't help but think about being inducted into the New York State Baseball Hall of Fame about 10 years ago. I had never really heard of it but was pleasantly surprised at the induction event and the reception from the people. It was nice being the first Met inducted, and since that time, the event had really grown and some of my old teammates like Swoboda, Hodges, Jones, and Agee have gone in.

The unique thing about this Hall of Fame is the diversity of its inductees. It's not only the pros that go in, but also nice mix of high school and college players, managers, and coaches. I understand they voted in a woman umpire and a woman player who played in *A League of Their Own* type of league and are always on the lookout for that under-the-radar type of person who made an impact on New York State baseball. And I've been told that its founder—Rene LeRoux—is working on creating an actual exhibit with artifacts and displays, sort of like Cooperstown. It kind of reminds me of the Mets from the early 1960s and how we grew over time into a championship team. It's worth checking out.

We had a party the night before Hodges was inducted that was sponsored by both the Mets and the Dodgers organizations. Steve Garvey spoke first about Hodges and, since I was the only one who knew him as a teammate and a manager, I spoke about my association with him as both. And I'm sure most of the people in the room that night knew something about my relationship with him. But it didn't matter if I was being redundant to what I'd said a thousand times before. Hodges made a difference. He was the leader we sorely needed. I've always said that the Mets would have won more championships with Hodges, and how sad it was for his family and the Mets organization when he died so young. But with all my physical issues, I've come to realize something more...that the time we had with Hodges was a gift, and we would not have won in '69 without him. And for that, I'm eternally grateful.

A few months later, we were back in New York for Old Timers' Day. I'd always enjoyed getting together with the guys for any old timers' games or reunions, and there'd been plenty of them. It had only been a few years since we came together to celebrate the '69 Mets 50th reunion. And it was then when I began thinking about my own mortality. You look around and you see who's passed, and that's the disappointing thing about these reunions. And there were guys who couldn't make it because they're too sick to come. Ron Taylor and Harrelson both have dementia, and other guys have died. It's tough to see your close friends and teammates have things happen to them. When I was waiting for my transplant, the thought I had was that I would become one of those guys. You're on the clock and you don't know what the outcome is going to be, and all you have is hope, so you get depressed during the waiting. But it's a great day to see them and to talk and forget about all that. Everyone has their problems. Everyone has their battles. So listening to the old war stories again jogs your memory quickly to all those good things that you did together.

This was much more than the usual gathering of guys to play a few innings before the real game. It was more of a reunion of all Mets teams, a blend of young and old. There were a handful of guys from that '69 team and a couple from '73. The team most represented was the '86 World Series team with about 18 guys. They invited all of us to the owners' box, and Steve Cohen introduced himself to everybody. The party was wonderful.

The next day when we made our way to the locker room to suit up there were so many guys that we had to have separate locker rooms. They had it separated by under 65 and over 65! When we went onto the field for introductions. I think it was great calling out the players by the team we played on. I came out with the '69 Mets, and we got a huge ovation. I could have gone out there 18 times, but I wanted to be with the '69 club.

Along with Jones, I was part of the committee that voted to retire Willie Mays' No. 24 and was sworn to secrecy until the announcement was made. There were 12 of us on the committee, including Howie Rose, Gary Cohen, Jay Horwitz, and others. Everyone knew the history of Joan Payson promising Mays she'd retire his number and that she'd passed away before she was able to honor that. And then as time went on and the new ownership ignored her promise to Mays, it looked like it would never happen.

I was there with Jones when she made that promise 50 years ago. I had my share of disappointment and setbacks and empty promises back then, so it came as no surprise to me that it didn't happen. But Horwitz was the guy who brought the subject up again, and Jones and I decided to help push it along. Jones was very vocal about retiring Mays' number and he took a hard stand in his defense. He respected him as a player and as a person and, like me, believed a promise was a promise.

On any committee you're gonna have some debate, and the only issue was that Mays played only two years as a Met. My thoughts on that whole issue were you're not retiring Mays for what he contributed to the Mets during that short time, but it was a goodwill gesture for the Giants and the Mets and what he did for baseball and to honor a promise. He was still representing New York.

I couldn't help but think about Mays playing so much of his career at Candlestick Park. You could see a guy like Juan Marichal or any other Giants pitcher standing on the mound, knowing the wind was blowing in a guy's face or swirling around, and usually both, and you knew as a hitter what you were up against. That was no different for Mays, and he still hit 660 home runs. Who knows how many balls he hit to the warning-track that would have gone out without that horrible wind? Put Mays in a better stadium and who knows how many more home runs he would have hit? Probably would have had more than Hank Aaron.

After the vote was made and the committee decided in favor of retiring Mays' number, I gave them the number of a guy who takes care of Mays and is a good friend of his. I'd remained close to Mays all these years later and I knew he was hurt because nothing had been done since Payson made her promise. He'd had surgery a few months earlier, so he was unable to attend, so he sent his son, Michael, to represent him.

They chose Jones, Felix Millan, Jon Matlack, and me to help unveil the giant "24" at the pitcher's mound. Of course, my thoughts were on Mays and what he did in his prime, what he did for his career. But my thoughts were more on the promise made by Payson and that Mays was alive to see this day. They say that time heals all wounds. I don't know if that's completely true, but the right thing to do was finally done.

When I arrived at the hotel for the old timers' get-together, the first guy I saw in the hotel lobby was Frank Thomas. It wasn't long after that when Jay Hook, Craig Anderson, and Ken MacKenzie, all pitchers from that '62 club, walked in together.

MacKenzie had been in the hospital earlier that day but wanted to be there so badly. I guess he pestered the hospital so much that they released him, and his son brought him to the ballpark. That weekend was all about the Mets, past and present. It was about Mays and Payson. It was about team and family and the importance of history.

But on an equally important level, that weekend was about guys like MacKenzie. It was about guys like him who played just a few years in a Mets uniform, and despite having physical issues and going against the doctor's orders, wouldn't miss something like this for the world. It was about Millan, whose career ended the way it did, and for Jones and what happened to him. It was for all the guys, from their points of view and what it means to be a Met.

As for me and the recalling of my story, I guess it's safe to say I was a survivor...a survivor in more ways than one. From never being traded to finding a kidney donor and then having my wife come through her surgery, I had my share of miracles both on and off the field. And as many times as I mentioned throughout this story that I was the odd man out, I look at things differently now. That with all the guys they traded for to play first base, none of them lasted as long as I did. I finally realized that I wasn't the odd man out. I was the odd man in.